## Country abbreviations

| | |
|---|---|
| **BEL.** | Belgium |
| **BOS. & HERZ.** | Bosnia and Herzegovina |
| **KOS.** | Kosovo (disputed) |
| **LIECH.** | Liechtenstein |
| **LUX.** | Luxembourg |
| **N. MAC.** | North Macedonia |
| **MON.** | Montenegro |
| **NETH.** | Netherlands |
| **NZ** | New Zealand |
| **SM** | San Marino |
| **SLVN.** | Slovenia |
| **SWITZ.** | Switzerland |
| **UAE** | United Arab Emirates |
| **UK** | United Kingdom |
| **US** | United States of America |
| **VAT. CITY** | Vatican City |

Gcl

# WHAT'S WHERE ON EARTH?

# ANIMAL
# ATLAS

# WHAT'S WHERE ON EARTH?

# ANIMAL ATLAS

## Derek Harvey

**Senior Editor** Jenny Sich
**Senior Art Editor** Rachael Grady
**Senior Cartographic Editor** Simon Mumford
**Senior Contributing Editors** Ashwin Khurana,
Anna Streiffert-Limerick
**Editor** Kelsie Besaw
**Designers** Vanessa Hamilton, Elaine Hewson,
Greg McCarthy, Lynne Moulding
**Illustrators** Jon @ KJA Artists, Adam Brackenbury,
Adam Benton, Arran Lewis, Kit Lane
**Creative Retoucher** Steve Crozier
**Managing Editor** Francesca Baines
**Managing Art Editor** Philip Letsu
**Production Editor** Gillian Reid
**Production Controller** Sian Cheung
**Jacket Designer** Akiko Kato
**Design Development Manager** Sophia MTT
**Picture Research** Myriam Megharbi, Sneha Murchavade,
Sakshi Saluja
**Publisher** Andrew Macintyre
**Associate Publishing Director** Liz Wheeler
**Art Director** Karen Self
**Publishing Director** Jonathan Metcalf

First published in Great Britain in 2021 by
Dorling Kindersley Limited
DK, One Embassy Gardens, 8 Viaduct Gardens,
London, SW11 7BW

The authorised representative in the EEA is
Dorling Kindersley Verlag GmbH. Arnulfstr. 124,
80636 Munich, Germany

Copyright © 2021 Dorling Kindersley Limited
A Penguin Random House Company
10 9 8 7 6 5 4 3 2 1
001–316690–Apr/2021

A CIP catalogue record for this book
is available from the British Library.
ISBN: 978-0-2414-1290-9

Printed and bound in the UAE

For the curious
www.dk.com

This book was made with Forest Stewardship Council™
certified paper – one small step in DK's commitment
to a sustainable future.
For more information go to
www.dk.com/our-green-pledge

# CONTENTS

**A WORLD OF ANIMALS**

**INVERTEBRATES**

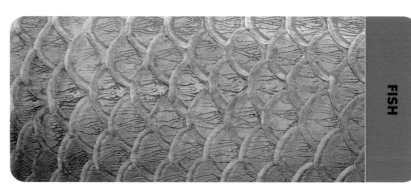

**FISH**

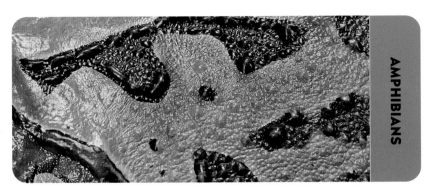

AMPHIBIANS

REPTILES

BIRDS

MAMMALS

# Foreword

This atlas of animals is about the living world, from the freezing poles to the tropical equator, from the highest mountain to the deepest sea. But this is no ordinary atlas because it shows where the animals live, as well as what they look like, and the forests, deserts, and oceans that are their homes.

Our planet is a very special part of our Solar System: it is the only one with life, and its breathtaking variety should fill us all with wonder. Animals of one kind or another survive almost everywhere on its surface, whether on land or underwater. Scientists have described more than 1.5 million species, and reckon there are many times this number still waiting to be discovered. Some, like the humpback whale or the osprey, range so far and wide that they span the entire globe. Others, like giant tortoises in the Galápagos Islands, live in less space than a single sprawling city. But all animals only succeed in places that supply what they need to survive and produce their babies, and many have very particular requirements. This means that koalas only live in Australia, where they eat eucalyptus leaves and nothing else, and parrotfish only swim in tropical coastal seas where they can munch on coral.

The animals in this book completely depend upon these wild places, but wilderness – the forests, grasslands, even unspoilt oceans – is disappearing. Since humans started building their civilizations

5,000 years ago, nearly two-thirds of the wilderness has gone. Cities have replaced trees, water and air have become polluted, and some animals have been hunted so much that very few are left. Many species have disappeared completely along with the wilderness, and others have been left threatened with extinction. This book tells the story of some of them – but also explains what is being done around the world to help. Today, more people than ever are concerned about the future of planet Earth and its extraordinary variety of animals. These animals are what make our world such an amazing place – we must look after them.

**Derek Harvey**

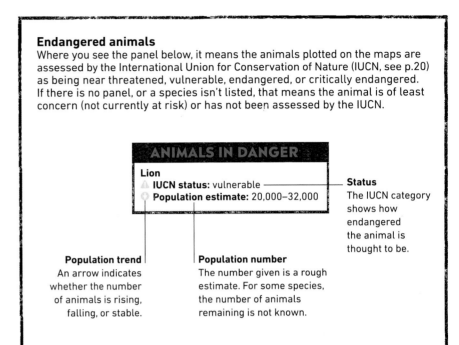

**Endangered animals**
Where you see the panel below, it means the animals plotted on the maps are assessed by the International Union for Conservation of Nature (IUCN, see p.20) as being near threatened, vulnerable, endangered, or critically endangered. If there is no panel, or a species isn't listed, that means the animal is of least concern (not currently at risk) or has not been assessed by the IUCN.

**ANIMALS IN DANGER**

Lion
⚠ IUCN status: vulnerable
⬆ Population estimate: 20,000–32,000

**Status**
The IUCN category shows how endangered the animal is thought to be.

**Population trend**
An arrow indicates whether the number of animals is rising, falling, or stable.

**Population number**
The number given is a rough estimate. For some species, the number of animals remaining is not known.

# A WORLD OF ANIMALS

# Amazing animals

Earth is teeming with life. Even places inhospitable to humans, such as the deepest oceans or hottest deserts, are alive with extraordinary animals. Wherever on the planet animals live, they have adaped to survive in their habitats.

**Polar bear**

**Birds**
Warm-blooded bodies and the power of flight mean that feathered birds have reached more parts of the world than any other group of land-living backboned animals, other than humans.

**Golden eagle**

**Bee hummingbird**

**Reptiles**
Like fishes and amphibians, reptiles are cold-blooded, relying on the Sun to warm their scaly bodies. They include crocodilians, turtles, lizards, and snakes.

## Variety of life

Animals are classified into major groups with shared characteristics: invertebrates, fish, amphibians, reptiles, birds, and mammals. Some of these groups contain more species than others, but all are represented around the world. Some are more widespread than others too: invertebrates exist almost everywhere, but reptiles do not inhabit the coldest places and amphibians do not reach remote islands.

**Marine iguana**

**King cobra**

**Adélie penguin**

**Antarctic krill**

**Housefly**

**Common toad**

**Mammals**
Humans are warm-blooded mammals, but we share this group with thousands of other species. All mammalian mothers produce milk to feed their babies and most mammals are covered in fur.

**Fish**
Half of all vertebrate species (animals with a backbone) are fish. Half live in saltwater oceans and half in freshwater lakes and rivers. They typically have a scaly body, fins for swimming, and gills for breathing underwater.

**Ladybird**

**Sailfish**

**Invertebrates**
These animals without a backbone make up the biggest animal group. They include worms, snails, insects, and many more. They live in every place capable of supporting animals.

**Cheetah**

**Monarch butterfly**

**Oarfish**

**Amphibians**
With their moist, scaleless skins, amphibians are mainly found in wet, freshwater habitats. They include frogs, toads, salamanders, newts, and worm-shaped caecilians.

**California sea lion**

**Red-eyed tree frog**

Every year, scientists discover and name new species of animals found across the world, from forests to coral reefs. As exciting as these finds are, experts believe that approximately 90 per cent of animal and plant species on Earth remain unknown. Listed below are some of the most recent amazing discoveries.

**Wasp mantis**
Found in the Peruvian Amazon in South America, this praying mantis has a body shape that makes it look like a stinging wasp. First described in 2019, it even moves and walks like a wasp, which helps to keep danger away.

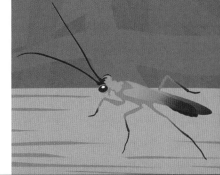

**Wakanda fairy wrasse**
This purple-and-blue fish from an East African coral reef reminded the scientists who first described it of the outfit worn by Marvel's Black Panther. So in 2019 they named it Wakanda, after the superhero's fictional African kingdom.

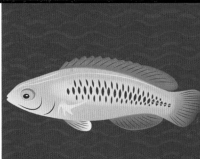

**Mini frogs**
Scientists who discovered three tiny Madagascan frogs, each smaller than a fingernail, described them in 2019. The three species are some of the smallest frogs found in the world and were called *Mini mum*, *Mini scule*, and *Mini ature*.

**Salazar's pit viper**
As fans of the Harry Potter books, the scientists who described this Indian snake in 2020 had a good option to name it. The venomous pit viper was named after the character Salazar Slytherin, who – in the story – could communicate with snakes.

**Alor myzomela**
Sadly, by the time they are named some new species are already under threat of extinction. Described in 2019, this striking bird – a honeyeater – located in eucalyptus forests on the Indonesian island of Alor is threatened by deforestation.

# Biomes

The same type of habitat, such as a desert or tropical rainforest, can occur in different parts of the world. These habitats – called biomes – look alike, even though different animals may live there. Each colour on this map represents a different land biome.

## Tundra

Close to the poles, conditions are so cold that the ground is frozen for much of the year, so few trees can grow. This open landscape, home to animals such as Arctic hares, is called the tundra.

## Mediterranean woodland

Woodland trees with thick, leathery leaves grow in places with warm, dry summers and mild winters, such as in the Mediterranean home of the asp viper, as well as in southern Africa and southern Australia.

## Taiga

Covering the largest land area is a stretch of cold, northern forest called taiga. It is dominated by evergreen coniferous trees, and is home to many animals, such as the wolverine, which range widely south of the Arctic.

## Temperate forest

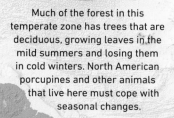

Much of the forest in this temperate zone has trees that are deciduous, growing leaves in the mild summers and losing them in cold winters. North American porcupines and other animals that live here must cope with seasonal changes.

## Ocean habitats

Conditions in ocean habitats are affected mainly by depths: animals living in deeper waters must cope with higher pressures, colder temperatures, and perpetual darkness.

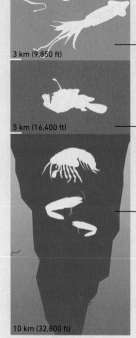

200 m (660 ft)

**Sunlit zone**
Here there is enough sunlight for algae – the "plants" of the ocean – to grow and support the underwater food chain. Most ocean life is found in the sunlit zone.

1 km (3,280 ft)

**Twilight zone**
It is too dark for algae to grow here, but just enough light reaches for animals to see. Many predatory fish live in the twilight zone.

3 km (9,850 ft)

**Midnight zone**
No light reaches below 1 km (3,280 ft), so many animals here produce their own light through a process called bioluminescence.

5 km (16,400 ft)

**Abyssal zone**
Near the cold, dark ocean floor, animals mostly rely on food sinking down from above.

**Hadal zone**
The ocean floor contains cracks called trenches that descend to nearly 10 km (32,800 ft). The pressures and temperatures in this zone are at their most extreme. Very specialized animals have adapted to live here.

10 km (32,800 ft)

## Temperate grassland

Grasslands usually grow when conditions are too dry for forest but too wet for desert. Temperate grasslands – home of the prairie chicken – are warm in summer and cold in winter, but stay green all year round.

## Tropical grassland

In the tropics, many grasslands are at their greenest during the rainy season. In places such as Africa, they support some of the biggest herds of hoofed mammals, including wildebeest, zebras, and giraffes.

# Where animals live

The world is made up of a variety of different habitats, from magnificent tropical forests and freezing, treeless tundras on land to colourful, sunlit coral reefs of the seas and cold, dark ocean depths. Each habitat has its own unique climate and supports its own ecosystem of plant and animal life.

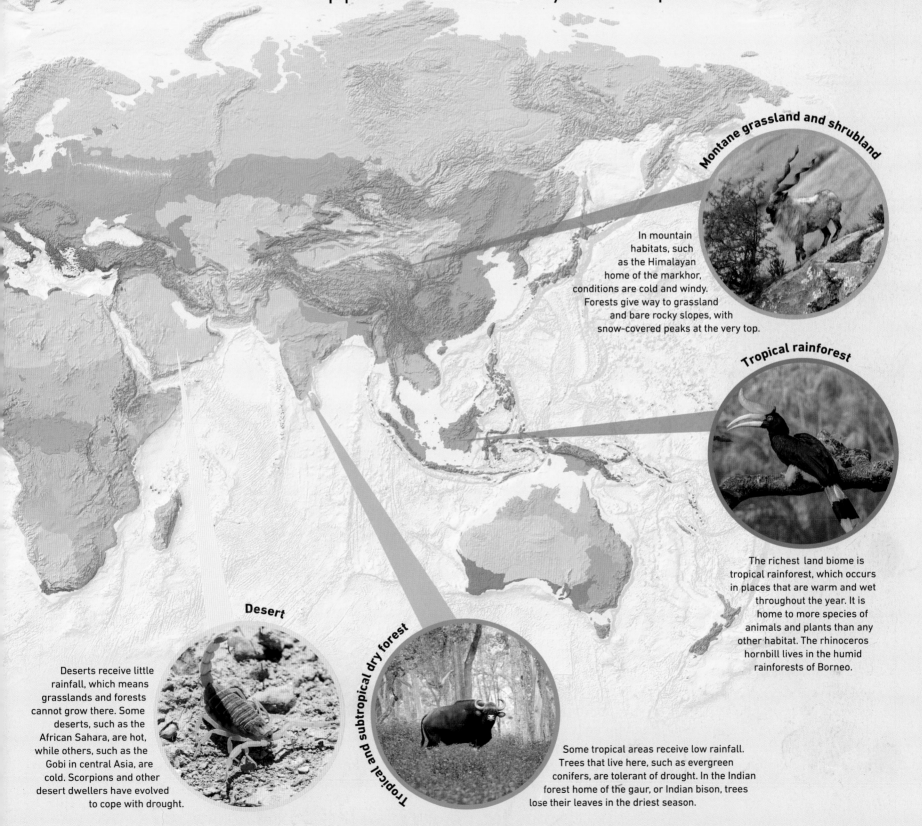

### Montane grassland and shrubland

In mountain habitats, such as the Himalayan home of the markhor, conditions are cold and windy. Forests give way to grassland and bare rocky slopes, with snow-covered peaks at the very top.

### Tropical rainforest

The richest land biome is tropical rainforest, which occurs in places that are warm and wet throughout the year. It is home to more species of animals and plants than any other habitat. The rhinoceros hornbill lives in the humid rainforests of Borneo.

### Desert

Deserts receive little rainfall, which means grasslands and forests cannot grow there. Some deserts, such as the African Sahara, are hot, while others, such as the Gobi in central Asia, are cold. Scorpions and other desert dwellers have evolved to cope with drought.

### Tropical and subtropical dry forest

Some tropical areas receive low rainfall. Trees that live here, such as evergreen conifers, are tolerant of drought. In the Indian forest home of the gaur, or Indian bison, trees lose their leaves in the driest season.

# Global origins

LAURASIA

GONDWANA

Over million of years, Earth has changed dramatically. Continents have split apart and crashed into each other, and large regions have flooded to create smaller islands. This has had an impact on where animals live today, sometimes leaving close cousins in different parts of the world.

## Changing Earth

Earth's outer layer, the crust, is split into tectonic plates, which move very slowly, carrying the land masses with them. Over billions of years, this slow movement has changed Earth's surface beyond recognition. This globe shows how Earth looked 300 million years ago, when the land was joined in two supercontinents called Gondwana and Laurasia.

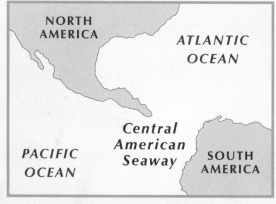

NORTH AMERICA

ATLANTIC OCEAN

PACIFIC OCEAN

*Central American Seaway*

SOUTH AMERICA

**North and South America more than 2.8 million years ago**

### Separated by sea

The Atlantic and Pacific oceans were once connected by a tropical ocean called the Central American Seaway. This body of water separated the continents of North and South America.

## Continental collision

Today, North and South America are joined by a narrow strip of land that formed 2.8 million years ago. Before this, animals on each continent were separated. When these two land masses collided, it created a passage for some animals to move across. Some animals from the north, including pumas, travelled south, and some from the south, such as armadillos, ventured north.

NORTH AMERICA

Puma

Armadillo

SOUTH AMERICA

Surinam toad

## Separated by flooding

Earth has experienced many ice ages, when large parts of the globe were covered with ice. When temperatures increased, melting ice caused sea levels to rise. Lots of islands around the world, like Sumatra and Borneo in Indonesia, formed in this way. In the process, animals there separated and evolved into different species, including the graceful pitta in Sumatra and blue-banded pitta in Borneo.

**Emerging islands**
When sea levels were lower, Sumatra, Borneo, and neighbouring islands were part of one land mass called the Sunda Shelf. With rising sea levels, much of the region became submerged (seen in a lighter colour), leaving behind islands.

**The Sunda Shelf in Southeast Asia about 20,000 years ago**

*Graceful pitta*

*Blue-banded pitta*

EUROPE

ASIA

AFRICA

*African clawed frog*

AUSTRALASIA AND OCEANIA

## Splitting up

South America and Africa were once joined, but started to drift apart 100 million years ago, separating animals. This explains why some animals are related, even with the vast Atlantic between them. One example is the Pipidae amphibians, which include South American Surinam toads and African clawed frogs.

**New ocean**
The matching shapes of South America and Africa is a clue that they were once joined. Volcanic activity in this area caused tectonic plates to move, pushing apart these land masses.

AFRICA

SOUTH AMERICA

**South America and Africa about 95 million years ago**

# **Under** threat

All around the world, animals are in decline and many species are facing extinction. As the human population grows bigger – using more space, eating more food, and polluting the environment – it becomes harder for animals to survive.

### **Biodiversity hotspots**

Some places on Earth are especially rich in plant and animal species. These biodiversity hotspots are highly vulnerable to threats such as deforestation and climate change because many of the species that live there are found nowhere else in the world. This map shows some of the world's most important hotspots, on land and in the sea.

### **Amazon rainforest**

The Amazon rainforest is a biodiversity hotspot containing thousands of species of insects, birds, and other animals, in a huge variety of different habitats. However, this spectacular South American region is under threat, mainly from the farming industry, which is clearing land for grazing cattle and to grow animal feed.

### **Rich habitat**

The bright, airy canopy of the rainforest is so different from the dense vegetation growing underneath, they are like two separate habitats – with different species of animals living in each.

### **Many species**

The Amazon rainforest is teeming with countless different creatures, from jaguars, anteaters, and colourful birds to tiny insects and not-so-tiny spiders. Many of the plant and animal species in this rich habitat rely on other species for things like food, shelter, and protection.

### **Declining wilderness**

Since the Industrial Revolution, when humans started burning more fuel for energy and clearing habitats on a scale greater than ever before, wild animals have lost more than 50 per cent of their living space. The wilderness has been converted to cities, farms, roads, and other developments.

*Bar chart: % OF WILD HABITAT REMAINING vs YEAR (1700, 1800, 1900, 2000). Scale 0 to 100.*

## Deforestation

Trees are felled to clear land for crops and livestock, or to develop buildings, dams, and open up mines. Their timber is also sold to make products, such as paper. An estimated 15 billion trees are cut down each year, resulting in the loss of forest habitats for animals and plants.

## Climate change

Burning fossil fuels, such as coal, releases carbon dioxide and other greenhouse gases into the atmosphere. The increasing levels of these gases is causing the world to warm up, threatening habitats on land and in the oceans, including the vital polar ice habitat of penguins.

## Building on the wilderness

When humans build towns, cities, and roads, they are carving up the wilderness to leave smaller and smaller patches of natural habitat. Some animals, such as predators that are high up in the food chain, need large areas in which to roam. They cannot survive in the isolated patches of habitat that remain.

## Poaching

Many kinds of wild animals are hunted for their meat, or because their bodies supply something that is considered valuable. Elephants have long been targeted for their ivory tusks, and rhinoceroses for their horns. This is illegal but it still takes place, driving some species to the edge of extinction.

## Overfishing

Some fish are under threat because so many are taken out of the ocean that their numbers cannot recover. Other species are caught up in nets and discarded as unwanted bycatch. The sharks pictured here have been targeted for their fins, considered a delicacy in some countries.

AN AREA OF **RAINFOREST** ALMOST THE **SIZE OF SWITZERLAND WAS LOST** DURING 2019 ALONE

 **OF MAMMALS ARE THREATENED BY EXTINCTION**

**Melting ice**
Climate change is heating up the Arctic quicker than anywhere else in the world. As sea ice melts, polar bears move onto land with limited access to seals, their primary food source. Without seals, polar bears are at real risk of starvation. If nothing is done, the global population of polar bears could halve to 10,000 by 2050.

# Conservation

Despite the threats that animals face, habitats are being saved and species brought back from the edge of extinction. Conservation schemes safeguard wildlife, by protecting wild areas or breeding rare species.

## Conservation in action

Today, national parks in Madgascar are helping to protect the critically endangered greater bamboo lemur – one of the world's rarest primates. Reduced habitat destruction, daily monitoring, and local educational programmes have been instituted to help save this rare species. This is just one example of how organizations all over the world have worked to save species since the 1960s.

**Distinctive tufts**
The greater bamboo lemur is recognizable by the white tufts around its ears.

## IUCN Red List

A global body called the International Union for the Conservation of Nature (IUCN) keeps a Red List of Threatened Species. Each of the more than 120,000 species listed is assigned a threat level in order to work out which ones need help most urgently.

**Rainforest reliance**
This species relies on rainforest where giant bamboo grows. The bamboo, which makes up 95 per cent of its diet, is being lost in forest clearance.

 **Least concern**
Unlikely to face extinction in the near future

 **Near threatened**
Close to a threat of extinction in the near future

 **Vulnerable**
Faces a high risk of extinction in the wild

 **Endangered**
Faces a very high risk of extinction in the wild

 **Critically endangered**
Faces an extremely high extinction risk in the wild

 **Extinct in the wild**
Survives only in captivity or far outside its natural range

 **Extinct**
Very likely that the last individual has died

## Species saved

Conservationists have used different methods to protect species from threats and help them recover, including setting aside protected wild areas, stopping hunting, or taking animals into captivity so they can breed safely there. Many species that were once on the brink of extinction have been saved, and today the populations of many of those species are growing.

**Flying high**
With a wingspan of 3 m (10 ft), the California condor soars to heights of up to 4,600 m (15,000 ft). It is the biggest flying bird in North America.

**California condor**
Hunting and lead poisoning helped to drive North America's biggest bird of prey to extinction in the wild in 1978. But captive breeding increased numbers, and birds could be released back into protected areas.

**Blue whale**
Once relentlessly hunted, the blue whale became one of the world's rarest species as its numbers plunged in the early 1900s. It is still endangered but, since a hunting ban in 1966, whale populations are now increasing.

**Mauritius kestrel**
In the 1970s, deforestation and introduced animals, such as mongooses and cats, meant that this island bird of prey was down to just four individuals – making it the world's rarest bird. They were taken into captivity for breeding, which has raised the population to hundreds.

**A horse apart**
Its stocky body, high mane, white nose, and shorter legs set the Przewalski's horse apart from domesticated horses.

**Przewalski's horse**
The world's only truly wild species of horse was hunted to extinction but survived in zoos, and today it is the focus of a captive breeding programme. In the 1990s, some were released back into their wild habitat in Mongolia.

**Sea otter**
The thick protective fur of the sea otter made this animal a target for hunters: it was hunted until there were just a thousand or so individuals left. A hunting ban and better protection of the seas helped it recover.

**100,000 NATIONAL PARKS AND WILDLIFE RESERVES EXIST IN THE WORLD TODAY**

 **OF EARTH'S LAND IS PROTECTED**

### Extinction in the wild

For some species in captivity, there is no true wild for them to return to. The last wild Père David's deer probably died in China more than 200 years ago, but some animals survived in a hunting park and were brought to England. The fenced herds alive today are all descended from these.

INVERTEBRATES

# Invertebrate facts

Tiny animals without backbones first appeared more than 600 million years ago. These early invertebrates lived in water, and many still do. Today, the diversity of invertebrates found throughout the world is staggering, from squids and starfish to worms and spiders.

## INVERTEBRATE **TYPES**

There are around 35 main groups of species in the animal kingdom. Just one of these groups, the vertebrates, contains all the fish, amphibians, reptiles, birds, and mammals. The other 34 groups are invertebrates – animals without an internal, jointed skeleton. Six of the main invertebrate groups are shown here.

**Sponges**
These primitive ocean organsims cannot move, and gather food by filtering it from the water.

**Cnidarians**
From jellyfish and anemones to corals, these sea creatures all have stinging tentacles to catch small prey.

**Echinoderms**
With their "spiny skin", these marine animals include starfish, sea cucumbers, and sea urchins.

**Molluscs**
From slugs to squids, molluscs live in damp habitats or in the sea. Many have a hard shell.

**Worms**
Found in water and on land, some – such as earthworms – are made up of many identical, soft-skinned segments.

**Arthropods**
With their tough outer skeletons and jointed legs, arthropods include insects, spiders, and crabs.

**ALMOST 97%** OF ALL ANIMALS ARE **INVERTEBRATES**.

## INVERTEBRATE **NUMBERS**

There are approximately 1.3 million known invertebrate species, but there could be many millions more. The vast majority of invertebrates belong to two groups: arthropods and molluscs.

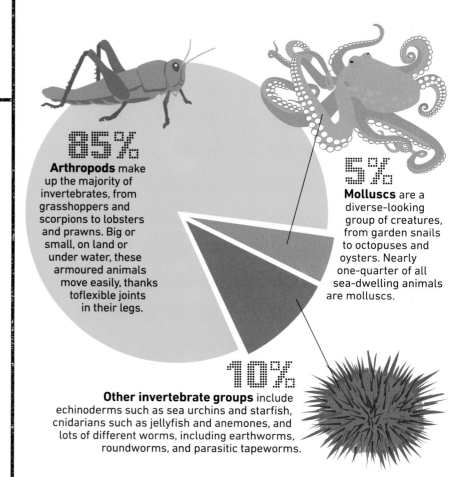

**85%**
**Arthropods** make up the majority of invertebrates, from grasshoppers and scorpions to lobsters and prawns. Big or small, on land or under water, these armoured animals move easily, thanks toflexible joints in their legs.

**5%**
**Molluscs** are a diverse-looking group of creatures, from garden snails to octopuses and oysters. Nearly one-quarter of all sea-dwelling animals are molluscs.

**10%**
**Other invertebrate groups** include echinoderms such as sea urchins and starfish, cnidarians such as jellyfish and anemones, and lots of different worms, including earthworms, roundworms, and parasitic tapeworms.

## **EXTREME** HABITATS

Some invertebrates can withstand – and even thrive – in incredibly hostile conditions, from barren, icy Antarctica to vast, unexplored regions thousands of metres below the ocean's surface.

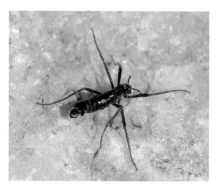

**Antarctic midges** are insects that measure only 1 cm (⅜ in), yet are the largest native land animal in Antarctica. They live at temperatures of -15°C (5°F), spending nine months of the year frozen solid.

**Tube worms**, a type of marine segmented worm, live on the Pacific Ocean seafloor near hydrothermal vents – volcanic areas where sections of Earth's crust are moving apart. They grow up to 3 m (10 ft).

# BODY **SHAPES**
Invertebrate body shapes fall into three main categories based on symmetry.

**Bilateral symmetry**
Many insects, from ladybirds to butterflies, have two halves that mirror each other.

**Radial symmetry**
Invertebrates such as starfish have several lines of symmetry around a central point.

**No symmetry**
Invertebrates like sponges have no lines of symmetry. They have irregular body shapes.

# SMART **OCTOPUS**
The coconut octopus uses tools, such as discarded coconuts or clam shells, to hide in while watching for prey such as crabs. Living on sandy bottoms in bays or lagoons in the western Pacific Ocean, this clever creature, which extends to about 15 cm (6 in), is also able to pick up and carry these tools more than 20 m (66 ft).

# **BIGGEST** INVERTEBRATE

**COLOSSAL SQUIDS** LIVE IN THE SOUTHERN OCEAN, AND CAN REACH **12**M (40 FT) LONG.

# **SMALLEST** INVERTEBRATE

Rotifer | Width of human hair

**ROTIFERS** ARE AMONG THE WORLD'S SMALLEST ANIMALS AT **0.05**MM (0.001 IN) LONG.

# FASTEST **INSECT**
The fastest insect relative to its body size is the tiger beetle. This 1.4 cm- (½ in-) long animal covers 120 times its body length in just a single second.

USAIN BOLT **OLYMPIC SPRINTER:** 5 BODY LENGTHS IN ONE SECOND

This long-legged creature runs so fast it temporarily goes blind from the speed.

**TIGER BEETLE:** 120 BODY LENGTHS IN ONE SECOND

# HIGHEST **JUMPER**

THE TINY **FROGHOPPER** CAN LEAP MORE THAN **60**CM (23 IN) IN THE AIR. THAT'S THE EQUIVALENT OF A **HUMAN JUMPING** **190 M (630 FT)**, OR A **40-STOREY BUILDING!**

# **HIGH** LIFE
THE **MOUNT EVEREST JUMPING SPIDER** LIVES UP TO **6,700**M (22,000 FT) ABOVE SEA LEVEL, ON THE SLOPES OF **MOUNT EVEREST**.

# LONGEST **MIGRATION**
THE **GLOBE SKIMMER DRAGONFLY** MIGRATES **7,080**KM (4,400 MILES) THROUGH THE AIR **WITHOUT LANDING**.

# BIGGEST **SWARM**
The desert locust gathers in swarms of up to 8 billion. Living in parts of the Middle East, Asia, and Africa, they are known to destroy crops.

# Giant Pacific octopus

ARCTIC OCEAN

Weighing as much as two grown men, the giant Pacific octopus is the largest of all octopus species, and one of the biggest ocean predators without a backbone. It is an agile, intelligent hunter, capable of catching prey as big as sharks.

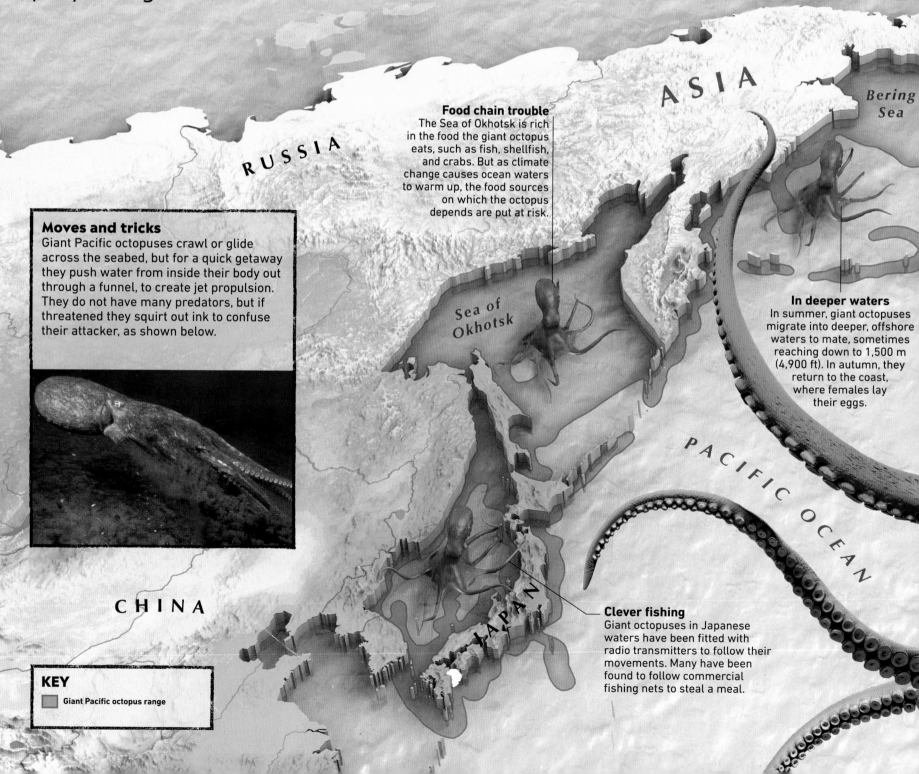

**Food chain trouble**
The Sea of Okhotsk is rich in the food the giant octopus eats, such as fish, shellfish, and crabs. But as climate change causes ocean waters to warm up, the food sources on which the octopus depends are put at risk.

**Moves and tricks**
Giant Pacific octopuses crawl or glide across the seabed, but for a quick getaway they push water from inside their body out through a funnel, to create jet propulsion. They do not have many predators, but if threatened they squirt out ink to confuse their attacker, as shown below.

**In deeper waters**
In summer, giant octopuses migrate into deeper, offshore waters to mate, sometimes reaching down to 1,500 m (4,900 ft). In autumn, they return to the coast, where females lay their eggs.

**Clever fishing**
Giant octopuses in Japanese waters have been fitted with radio transmitters to follow their movements. Many have been found to follow commercial fishing nets to steal a meal.

ASIA

RUSSIA

Bering Sea

Sea of Okhotsk

PACIFIC OCEAN

CHINA

JAPAN

**KEY**
Giant Pacific octopus range

## Cold-water hunter

A big speedy predator, the giant Pacific octopus thrives in the cold, oxygen-rich waters around the northern rim of the Pacific Ocean, mostly in seas that are rarely deeper than 500 m (1,640 ft). The octopus grabs prey with its arms, then uses its beak to inject venom into the prey. This immobilizes the prey and softens its flesh, which the octopus then can lick out with its rasping tongue.

### Octopus nursery
Each female octopus lays up to 100,000 eggs in an underwater cave or crevice. She guards the eggs, which hang in clutches, until they hatch about six months later and she dies. The tiny hatchlings then spend about two months drifting among the ocean's plankton, before descending to the seabed, where they develop into adult shape and size.

NORTH AMERICA

CANADA

USA

Aleutian Islands

### Fleshy body
The thick wrinkly skin of a giant Pacific octopus covers a soft, fleshy body that can squeeze through the smallest gaps. This is useful for catching prey hiding in crevices or escaping enemies on a rocky reef.

### Northern range
Furthest north, most giant octopuses live in shallower waters. Many live in coastal reefs and some may even drift into the intertidal zone by the shore.

### Accidental catch
In the rich fishing waters of the northeast Pacific, giant Pacific octopuses risk being caught in nets cast for cod and flatfish. It is the octopus species most commonly landed as a bycatch here.

PACIFIC OCEAN

A **GIANT PACIFIC OCTOPUS** CAN WEIGH **180 KG** (400 LB) AND ITS LONG ARMS CAN **SPAN UP TO 6 M** (20 FT)

### Strong arms
Octopuses have eight arms that carry two rows of large suckers for gripping prey. Each arm can have more than 500 suckers in total.

# European lobster

Lobsters are crustaceans, a group of invertebrates with armour-like, jointed exoskeletons protecting their soft bodies. One of the largest lobster species, the European lobster lives in shallow coastal seas across most of Europe and northern Africa.

**North Sea**
The North Sea is the biggest expanse of shallow continental waters in the northeast Atlantic. It is rich in lobsters' favourite food, such as crabs, starfish, and sea urchins.

North Sea

**Long antennae**
Lobsters use their antennae to feel their way around on the seabed in murky, dark waters.

ATLANTIC OCEAN

**Warmer waters**
Like many European marine species, the European lobster reaches the southern limits of its range in the waters off the coast of Morocco in northwest Africa. It cannot tolerate the warmer tropical seas further south.

**The Azores**
This group of small volcanic islands marks the westernmost part of the European lobster's territory.

**Uneven-sized claws**
The fatter claw of a lobster is stronger for slow crushing, while the slimmer one is better for faster cutting. Both are used for breaking up food or in self-defence.

## Lobster movements
Most lobsters migrate into deeper waters to spawn, but one of the most spectacular migrations happens every autumn off the coast of America, when huge numbers of spiny lobsters move in single file over the seabed to reach their spawning grounds.

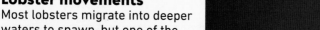

**KEY**

European lobster range

ARCTIC OCEAN

## Norwegian Sea
Warm ocean currents flowing up from the tropical Atlantic into the Norwegian Sea help to keep waters ice-free, so lobsters live as far north as the Arctic Circle.

## Life on the seabed
A lobster needs water to help support its weighty body, which is far too heavy for the lobster to move around on rocky shores or beaches. Lobsters mostly crawl across the seabed, where they live in crevices or burrows. When needed, they escape by quickly swimming backwards. Even a big lobster might be swept away by strong currents in deeper water, so they don't go too far offshore.

## Coastal crustacean
Like many other marine animals, the European lobster stays mainly in coastal seas. Lobsters are fished for food, but despite some local overfishing, especially in the North Sea, the overall population is stable.

## Black Sea
Rivers flowing into the cool Black Sea make it less salty than the ocean. European lobsters can survive here, but in fewer numbers and only in western areas.

Baltic Sea

EUROPE

Black Sea

Crete

Mediterranean Sea

## Eastern Mediterranean
The Mediterranean Sea reaches a depth of over 5,000 m (16,400 ft) in the middle. Lobsters keep to shallower coastal waters, ranging as far east as the Greek island of Crete.

## Salty environment
A warm climate evaporates water from the Mediterranean Sea and makes it slightly saltier than the Atlantic Ocean. Lobsters can take these conditions, and range widely across this region.

AFRICA

FEMALE **EUROPEAN LOBSTERS** CAN LIVE UP TO **THE AGE OF** 70

**OVERFISHING** IN THE **NORTH SEA** HAS MADE **LOBSTER NUMBERS** THERE **DROP BY** 90%

### Caterpillar diet

Postman butterflies become poisonous very early in their life. Their caterpillars eat leaves of passion vines, which contain toxic cyanide. The poison stays in their bodies without harming them, even as they turn into butterflies. Adults also only feed on passion vines, but on the nectar and pollen of its flowers.

### Guiana Highlands

In this area of tabletop mountains rising steeply from rainforests, the butterflies have little or no white in their colour pattern – similar to those of the Andean mountains.

### Central America

In the rainforests from Guatemala to Panama, postman butterflies have red bands on their forewings and white bands, sometimes tinged with yellow, on their hindwings.

### Andes

High up in the mountain valleys and foothills of the northern Andes range, the butterflies' hindwings have less white; some have no white in their pattern at all.

*Guiana Highlands*

*Amazon*

### Regional colours

Some species of butterfly have many different varieties according to where they live. The postman butterfly, for example, has more than 20 variations. Some of these are shown on this map, in the areas where they live.

# Postman butterfly

The postman butterfly lives in varied habitats from Central to South America. Across its range, its exact pattern of red, black, and white varies from place to place. A flash of colour from any postman butterfly is a sign that it is poisonous, so helps to keep predatory birds away.

THERE ARE ABOUT **20,000 SPECIES OF BUTTERFLY** IN THE **WORLD**

**AT NIGHT,** POSTMAN BUTTERFLIES GATHER TO **SLEEP IN GROUPS** KNOWN AS **COMMUNAL ROOSTS**

**Amazon Basin**
Across the lowlands of the great Amazon River Basin, local postman butterflies often live along rivers and streams. Here, they have white patches on their forewings, sometimes broken into spots.

**Wings at rest**
Like most day-flying butterflies, postman butterflies rest with their wings raised so their tips almost touch. Flapping their wings helps to spread a scent that deters predators.

**Master mimics**
Closely related to the postman butterfly, the red postman (above) is a separate species, but matches the local colour pattern of the postman wherever it lives alongside it. As they are both poisonous, this mimicry reinforces the warning for potential predators and helps both species survive.

**KEY**

◻ Postman butterfly range

**Wetlands**
In Brazil's Pantanal wetlands, the postman lives near water. Here it has white stripes on the hindwings, looking more like those along Brazil's southwest coast and in Central America.

Amazon Basin

SOUTH AMERICA

Andes

**Sucking nectar**
Butterflies have a flexible tube called a proboscis for drinking liquid nectar from flowers. Usually kept coiled up, it unrolls when the butterfly is ready to feed.

**Passion flower**

**Wing pattern**
The colours of the postman butterfly come from tiny pigmented scales that cover the surface of the two pairs of wings. Its wingspan can measure up to 7.5 cm (3 in).

## Plant pollinator

Bees are essential for keeping our planet green. They transfer pollen from flower to flower, pollinating many crops that we depend on for food. This mining bee is busy harvesting pollen from an apple blossom tree in Wisconsin, USA. But climate change is affecting bee behaviour, and intensive farming and pesticides are destroying bee habitats, such as wildflower meadows, trees, and hedgerows.

**THE OLDEST MEXICAN RED-KNEED TARANTULA IS KNOWN TO HAVE LIVED FOR**

## 28

**YEARS**

**GOLIATH TARANTULA FANGS CAN GROW UP TO**

## 3.8 CM
(1½ IN)

**Western desert tarantula**
One of the largest spiders in North America, this desert species from Arizona and Mexico survives heat and drought by burrowing underground.

NORTH AMERICA

**Mighty spiders**
Tarantulas grow bigger and live longer than other spiders. In most parts of the tropics they are high in the food chain. But their numbers are small wherever they live, making them vulnerable to habitat destruction.

**Mexican red-kneed tarantula**
Found in tropical hill forests, this species burrows into banks and around tree roots. A popular pet, it is now threatened by illegal trade.

SOUTH AMERICA

AFRICA

**Goliath tarantula**
The biggest tarantula – and heaviest spider of them all – lives in the rainforests of the Amazon basin. It has a legspan of 30 cm (12 in).

**Chaco golden-kneed tarantula**
The Chaco is an area of extensive grassland in South America, south of the Amazon, and the golden-kneed is one of many tarantula species that thrive in this habitat.

**Blue-footed baboon spider**
Baboon spiders are ground-living tarantulas found in Africa. They get their name from their wide-tipped legs, which are said to resemble the fingers of a baboon.

# Tarantulas

Many big spiders are called "tarantulas", but all true tarantulas have fat hairy bodies and belong to a family called the theraphosids. Found in all warm parts of the world, there are nearly 1,000 species: the smallest is no bigger than your thumb, but the biggest can span a large dinner plate with its legs.

**Venomous fangs**
Spiders use their fangs to inject venom that disables their prey. Tarantula venom can be deadly to small creatures, but is usually no more serious to a human than a bee sting.

**Mexican red-kneed tarantula**

**Hairy legs**
All spiders have hairs or bristles, but tarantulas are hairier than most. Many hairs are touch-sensitive, used in detecting movement of prey. In American species, such as this one, they are barbed to irritate and can be scattered in self-defence.

EUROPE

ASIA

**Indian tree tarantula**
One of many species of climbing tarantulas, this spider with striking markings lives in tree holes, where it mainly preys on large insects.

**Ambush tactics**
Tarantulas ambush prey, rather than trapping them in webs. The largest ones are big enough to kill small vertebrates; in this photo, two Peruvian tarantulas are feeding on a treefrog.

AUSTRALIA

**Queensland whistling spider**
Like some other Australian tarantulas, the whistling spider makes a hissing sound to deter predators, by rubbing stiff bristles at the base of its fangs.

**KEY**
☐ Combined range of all species of tarantula

**Spiny skin**
Protective spines grow from small hard plates just under the skin.

**Smell sensors**
The skin contains sensitive chemical receptors that pick up the faintest scent of prey.

**Simple eyes**
An eyespot at the tip of each arm allows the starfish to detect light and shade.

*Greenland*

*Labrador Sea*

NORTH AMERICA

## Atlantic star

The common starfish is found along the Atlantic coasts of North America and Europe, down to depths of 400 m (1,300 ft). When food is abundant, especially in spring and summer, they appear in huge numbers along these coastlines.

**Colder coasts**
Common starfish cannot survive and breed in waters as cold as the Arctic, but warm currents flowing up from the equator help push their natural range north, along parts of Greenland's coast.

*Newfoundland*

*Bermuda*

**Ocean mixing**
Starfish on North America's Atlantic coast are regarded as the same species as those in Europe. Currents in the North Atlantic help mix starfish larvae from both sides of the ocean.

**Mid-ocean realm**
A population of starfish lives along the rocky shores, reefs, and sandbanks around the Azores, a group of volcanic islands far out in the Atlantic.

*Azores*

ATLANTIC OCEAN

**Starfish larvae**
Starfish begin their life as eggs, hatching into tiny larvae that drift among minute organisms called plankton, on which they feed. Older larvae (seen here) develop sticky arms that they use to attach to the seabed, before growing their five adult spiny arms.

IF ONE OF THE **STARFISH'S FIVE LIMBS** IS **SEVERED**, IT SIMPLY **GROWS ONE BACK**

# Common starfish

Along with sea cucumbers and urchins, the common starfish belongs to a group of animals called echinoderms, which live only in the ocean. Like many marine animals commonly spotted on or near the seashore, the starfish actually spends most of its life in deeper waters, as it needs to be underwater to spawn.

ARCTIC OCEAN

Svalbard

**Many tiny feet**
Like other echinoderms, starfish move from place to place using tiny sucker-like tube feet. The underside of their arms is covered in hundreds of these feet, which bend from side to side to push the animal slowly along the seafloor.

**Norwegian fjords**
Norway's long coastline is carved by narrow, deep inlets called fjords. The muddy and sandy bottoms of these coastal habitats are full of common starfish.

**Northern delights**
Even along the Kola Peninsula, above the Arctic Circle, warm currents keep waters ice-free. Here, starfish feed on the plentiful scallop-beds.

Iceland

Faroe islands

North Sea

Baltic Sea

Kola Peninsula

Rockall Banks

**Colours**
The skin of the common starfish is usually orange, but some are in shades of brown or purple.

EUROPE

**North Sea water**
The North Sea is slightly less salty than the open ocean because many rivers flow into it. Common starfish still thrive here, even in river estuaries.

**The Baltic Sea**
The common starfish is one of the few echinoderms that can survive in the very low salt levels of the Baltic.

**Mussels on the menu**
The common starfish preys on lots of different invertebrates, but has a special liking for two-shelled molluscs, such as mussels. They pull the shells apart with their arms, then stick their extendible stomach through the opening to digest the meat inside.

AFRICA

**KEY**
 Common starfish range

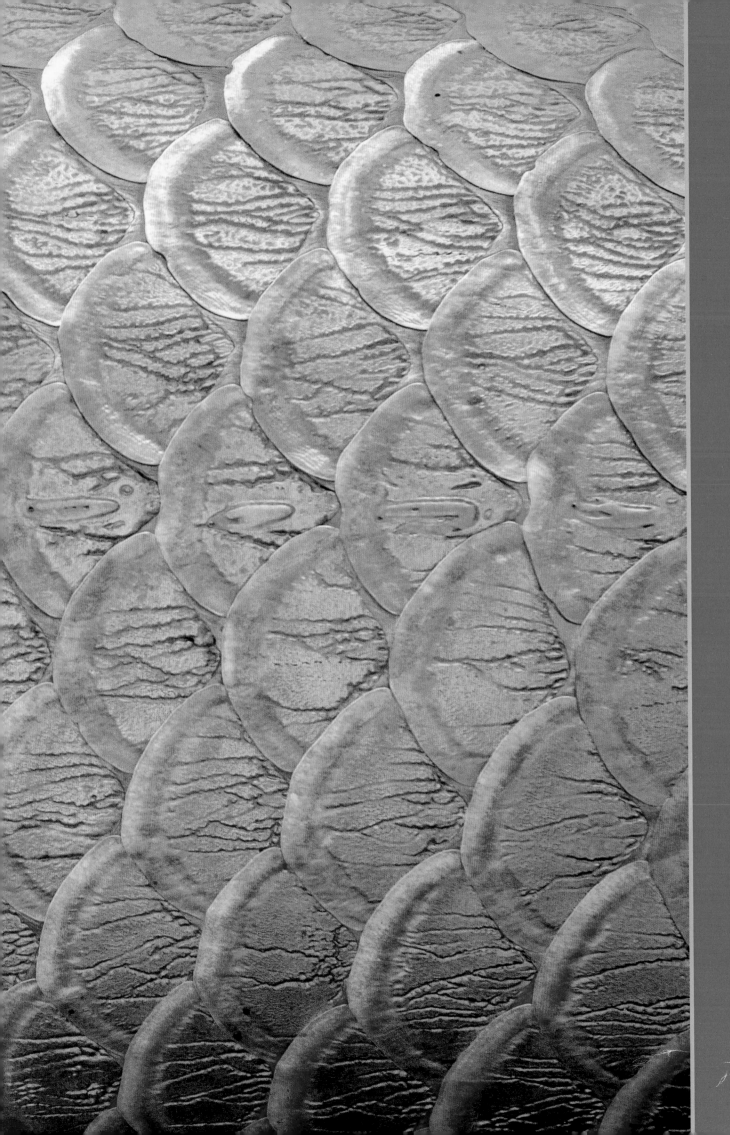

FISH

# Fish facts

Fish evolved more than 500 million years ago, and were the first animals to evolve a backbone. They can be found in a variety of places, from vast oceans to small freshwater lakes. Some fish live on bright coral reefs, while others lurk thousands of metres deeper in pitch-black oceanic trenches.

## WHAT IS A FISH?

**Vertebrates**
The typical fish skeleton consists of a spinal column, skull, ribs, and fin supports.

**Cold-blooded**
Fish may swim in warm or cold water, but their bodies are the same temperature as the water they live in.

**Breathe with gills**
Gills located on the side of a fish contain blood that absorbs oxygen from the water.

**Scaly skin**
Most fish are covered in protective, overlapping plates called scales. Some fish do not have scales.

**Live in water**
Some fish swim in salty oceans, others need fresh water to survive. Some move between the two.

## FISH TYPES

**ESTIMATED NUMBER OF FISH SPECIES:** 35,660

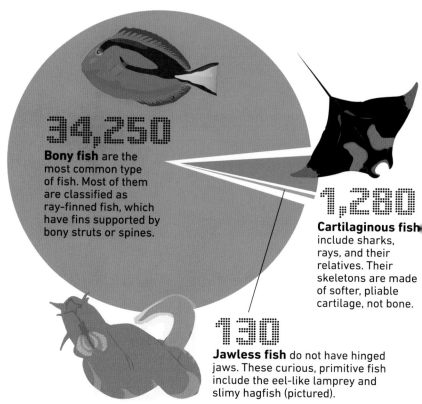

**34,250**
**Bony fish** are the most common type of fish. Most of them are classified as ray-finned fish, which have fins supported by bony struts or spines.

**1,280**
**Cartilaginous fish** include sharks, rays, and their relatives. Their skeletons are made of softer, pliable cartilage, not bone.

**130**
**Jawless fish** do not have hinged jaws. These curious, primitive fish include the eel-like lamprey and slimy hagfish (pictured).

THE **GULF CORVINA** IS THE LOUDEST FISH — WITH A CALL OF 202 DECIBELS, IT'S **LOUDER THAN A PLANE TAKING OFF!**

## EXTREME HABITATS

Some fish have evolved to survive in the most inhospitable of conditions, from the frozen Arctic to dried-up riverbeds.

**Arctic cod** can survive in sub-zero temperatures, using an anti-freeze protein in their blood. This allows them to find food beneath the ice in polar regions, without any competition.

**Mudskippers** are found in the Indian and Pacific oceans, but they actually prefer the land – and even climb trees! They can keep on breathing on land for up to two days at a time.

**Lungfish** live in rivers and lakes in Africa, Australia, and South America. During dry seasons, they burrow into mud, before cocooning themselves in a mucus that traps life-saving moisture.

## LONGEST MIGRATION

**DORADO CATFISH** MIGRATE 11,600 KM (7,200 MILES) INLAND, FROM THE ANDES TO THE AMAZON AND BACK.

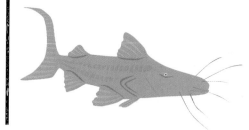

# SWIMMING LIKE A FISH

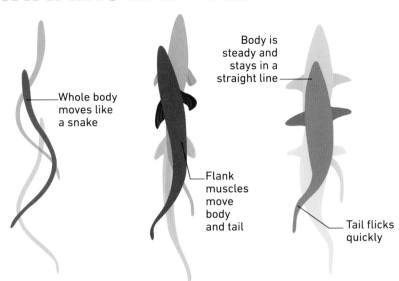

- Whole body moves like a snake
- Body is steady and stays in a straight line
- Flank muscles move body and tail
- Tail flicks quickly

**Side to side**
Long, thin fish, such as eels, propel themselves using a series of fast S-shaped movements through the water.

**Body and tail**
Many fish, including salmon, swim with the help of their body and tail, using their powerful flank muscles to move forwards.

**Strong tail**
The fastest fish, from tuna to sharks, maintain a straight, streamlined body, while their flank muscles flick their tail from side to side.

# SMALLEST FISH

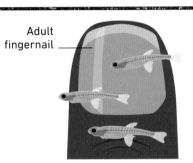

Adult fingernail

*PAEDOCYPRIS PROGENETICA* IS THE SMALLEST-KNOWN FISH, WITH FEMALES MEASURING JUST

**7.9** MM (5/16 in).

# ENDEMIC SPECIES

Some fish are native to a specific habitat and do not stray from there – they are endemic to that region. This is because these fish have evolved to adapt in that area only, and they cannot survive for long anywhere else.

**Coelacanths** were thought to be extinct for 65 million years, but in 1938 scientists discovered them off the coast of south-eastern Africa. Since then, an Indonesian coelacanth has also been found.

**Elephantnose fish** are a curious-looking freshwater species native to western and central Africa. They are found in slow-moving rivers and muddy pools.

# DEEPEST FISH

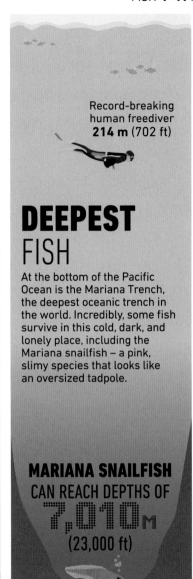

Record-breaking human freediver **214 m** (702 ft)

At the bottom of the Pacific Ocean is the Mariana Trench, the deepest oceanic trench in the world. Incredibly, some fish survive in this cold, dark, and lonely place, including the Mariana snailfish – a pink, slimy species that looks like an oversized tadpole.

**MARIANA SNAILFISH** CAN REACH DEPTHS OF **7,010**M (23,000 ft)

# BIGGEST FISH

WHALE SHARKS GROW **12**M (40 FT) LONG – ABOUT THE SAME LENGTH AS A BUS.

# SMART FISH

Found in the Indian and Pacific oceans, the reef-dwelling tuskfish can use a rock to smash open shellfish, making it the first wild fish observed using tools.

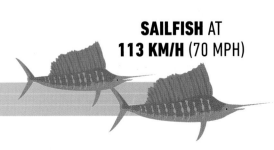

# FASTEST FISH

Named for their spectacular dorsal fin, sailfish would easily win a race against the fastest human swimmer. They live in the warm Atlantic and Indo-Pacific waters.

MICHAEL PHELPS **OLYMPIC SWIMMER** AT **7.6 KM/H** (4.7 MPH)

**SAILFISH** AT **113 KM/H** (70 MPH)

# Sea lamprey

The sea lamprey is a jawless fish – instead of jaws it has a sucker filled with teeth, which it uses to feed on the blood of other fishes. It grows up as a larva in the rivers and lakes of North America and Europe, then lives its adult life in the salty North Atlantic Ocean, before returning to freshwater habitats to breed and die.

**Northern waters**
Sea lampreys can be found all across the North Atlantic, from the frigid waters of Greenland to the balmy latitudes of Spain and Florida, USA. While most adults live in the ocean, some make the Great Lakes of North America their home all year round.

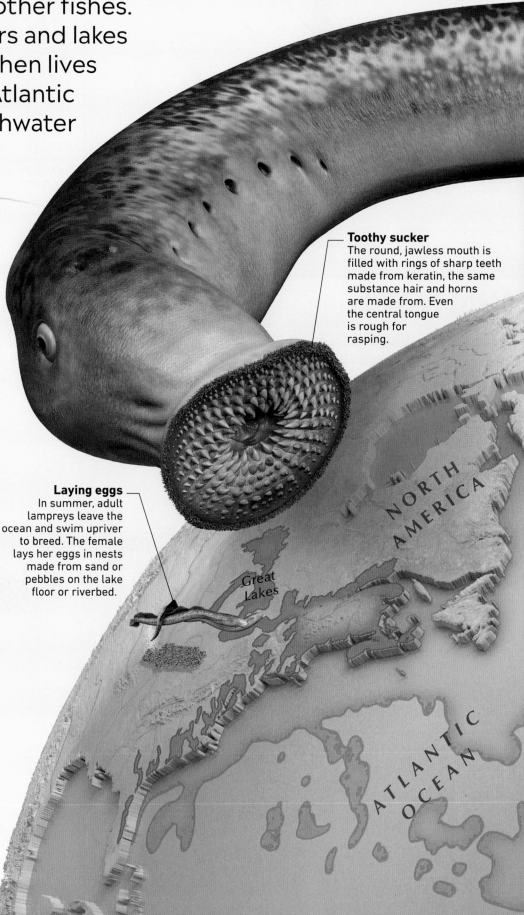

**Toothy sucker**
The round, jawless mouth is filled with rings of sharp teeth made from keratin, the same substance hair and horns are made from. Even the central tongue is rough for rasping.

**Laying eggs**
In summer, adult lampreys leave the ocean and swim upriver to breed. The female lays her eggs in nests made from sand or pebbles on the lake floor or riverbed.

Great Lakes

NORTH AMERICA

ATLANTIC OCEAN

**Lamprey larvae**
Sea lamprey eggs hatch into young called larvae. The larvae burrow into gravel on the riverbed, leaving their heads exposed. They filter feed on tiny particles swept into their mouth by tiny microscopic hairs called cilia. This larval phase can last for up to three years.

**Feeding on blood**
Adult lampreys clamp fast to other fish with their sucker-like mouths to feed. They use their horny teeth and tongue to cut a hole in the prey's skin, swallowing its blood as food. The lamprey's saliva stops the blood clotting so it keeps flowing, often until the victim dies.

 ONE **SPAWNING** FEMALE **SEA LAMPREY** MAY LAY UP TO **300,000 EGGS**

THE **LENGTH** OF A **SEA LAMPREY** CAN BE UP TO  **1.2m** (4 FT)

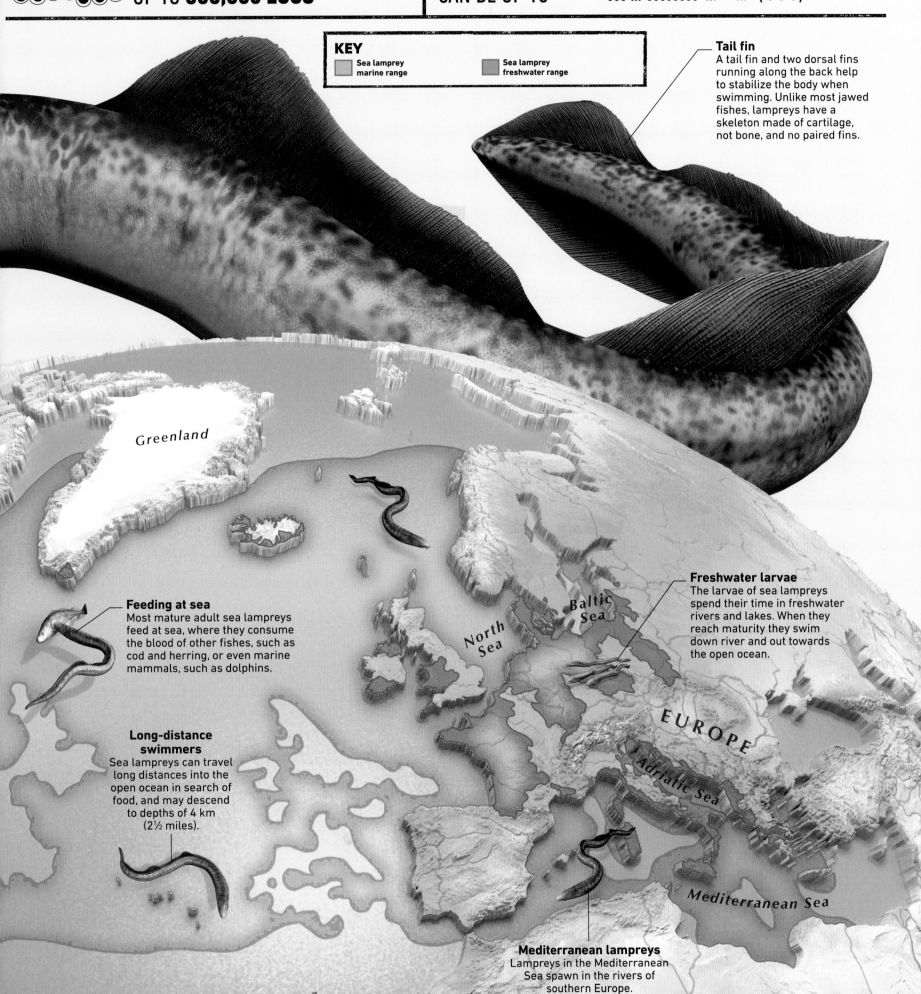

**KEY**

Sea lamprey marine range

Sea lamprey freshwater range

**Tail fin**
A tail fin and two dorsal fins running along the back help to stabilize the body when swimming. Unlike most jawed fishes, lampreys have a skeleton made of cartilage, not bone, and no paired fins.

*Greenland*

**Feeding at sea**
Most mature adult sea lampreys feed at sea, where they consume the blood of other fishes, such as cod and herring, or even marine mammals, such as dolphins.

**Long-distance swimmers**
Sea lampreys can travel long distances into the open ocean in search of food, and may descend to depths of 4 km (2½ miles).

*North Sea*

*Baltic Sea*

**Freshwater larvae**
The larvae of sea lampreys spend their time in freshwater rivers and lakes. When they reach maturity they swim down river and out towards the open ocean.

EUROPE

*Adriatic Sea*

*Mediterranean Sea*

**Mediterranean lampreys**
Lampreys in the Mediterranean Sea spawn in the rivers of southern Europe.

# Great white shark

Armed with razor-sharp teeth and a sleek body shaped like a torpedo, the great white shark is a fast, formidable predator. This wanderer roams throughout the world's oceans, but returns to the coast to hunt marine mammals such as seals, dolphins, and even small whales.

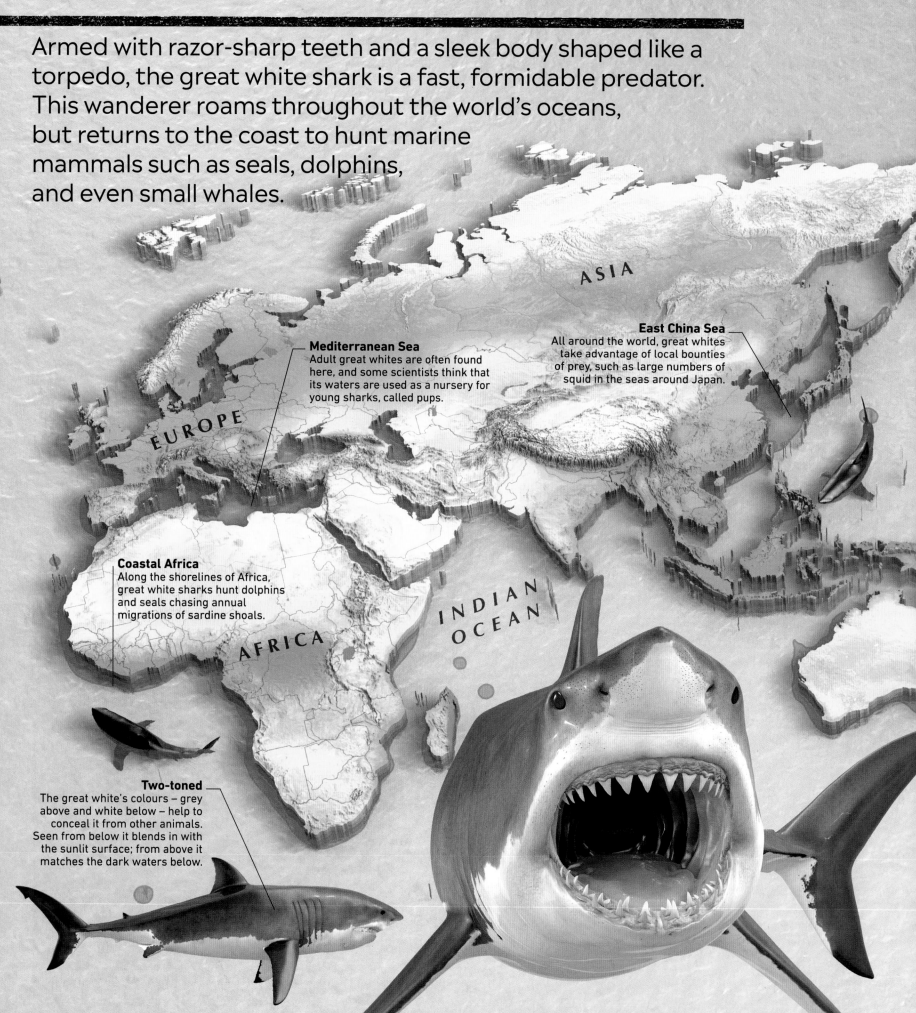

**Mediterranean Sea**
Adult great whites are often found here, and some scientists think that its waters are used as a nursery for young sharks, called pups.

**East China Sea**
All around the world, great whites take advantage of local bounties of prey, such as large numbers of squid in the seas around Japan.

**Coastal Africa**
Along the shorelines of Africa, great white sharks hunt dolphins and seals chasing annual migrations of sardine shoals.

**Two-toned**
The great white's colours – grey above and white below – help to conceal it from other animals. Seen from below it blends in with the sunlit surface; from above it matches the dark waters below.

ASIA

EUROPE

AFRICA

INDIAN OCEAN

**KEY**

☐ Great white shark range

## Tracking sharks

Little is known about the exact movements of great whites, but they can be followed by fitting them with tracking devices. These transmit signals to satellites, which send information back to Earth about the animal's location. Such studies show they travel thousands of kilometres across the oceans.

NORTH AMERICA

## The Caribbean islands

Great whites typically stick to cooler waters, but sometimes they seek prey in tropical seas, such as in the Caribbean and Gulf of Mexico.

Gulf of Mexico

ATLANTIC OCEAN

SOUTH AMERICA

PACIFIC OCEAN

## North Pacific

Underwater mountain chains in this region may provide great whites a habitat rich with prey, extending their range further west from the USA.

PACIFIC OCEAN

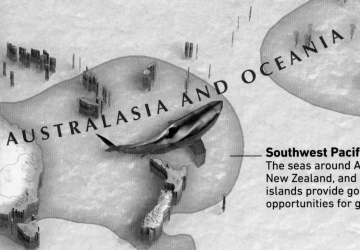

AUSTRALASIA AND OCEANIA

## Southwest Pacific

The seas around Australia, New Zealand, and neighbouring islands provide good hunting opportunities for great whites.

## Southeast Pacific

In this wide range great white sharks can follow long "highways" that take them far into the open waters.

## South Atlantic coast

Many great whites live permanently in this region, where their warm-bloodedness helps them hunt in colder waters.

## Ruthless killer

Once a great white shark sights a target near the water's surface, it moves in quickly for the kill. It attacks its prey, such as this sea lion, with a single ferocious bite – and in the process can breach the surface in spectacular fashion. It then lets the victim bleed to death before starting to feed.

## Long-distance wanderer

The great white shark is the world's widest-ranging fish and can be found in most oceans, but is found most often in the ranges shown on this map. Unusually for a fish, it maintains a high body temperature, helping it to survive in colder waters and chase down warm-blooded mammals.

 A **GREAT WHITE SHARK** CAN HAVE UP TO **300 TEETH**

## Shallow waters

In the sunlit waters of the Maldives in the Indian Ocean, blacktip reef sharks are rounding up their prey. Forcing the fish into ever denser shoals, they nudge them into shallow water close to the shore before moving in to take a bite. These agile hunters are found in all shallow tropical seas, particularly around coral reefs and lagoons.

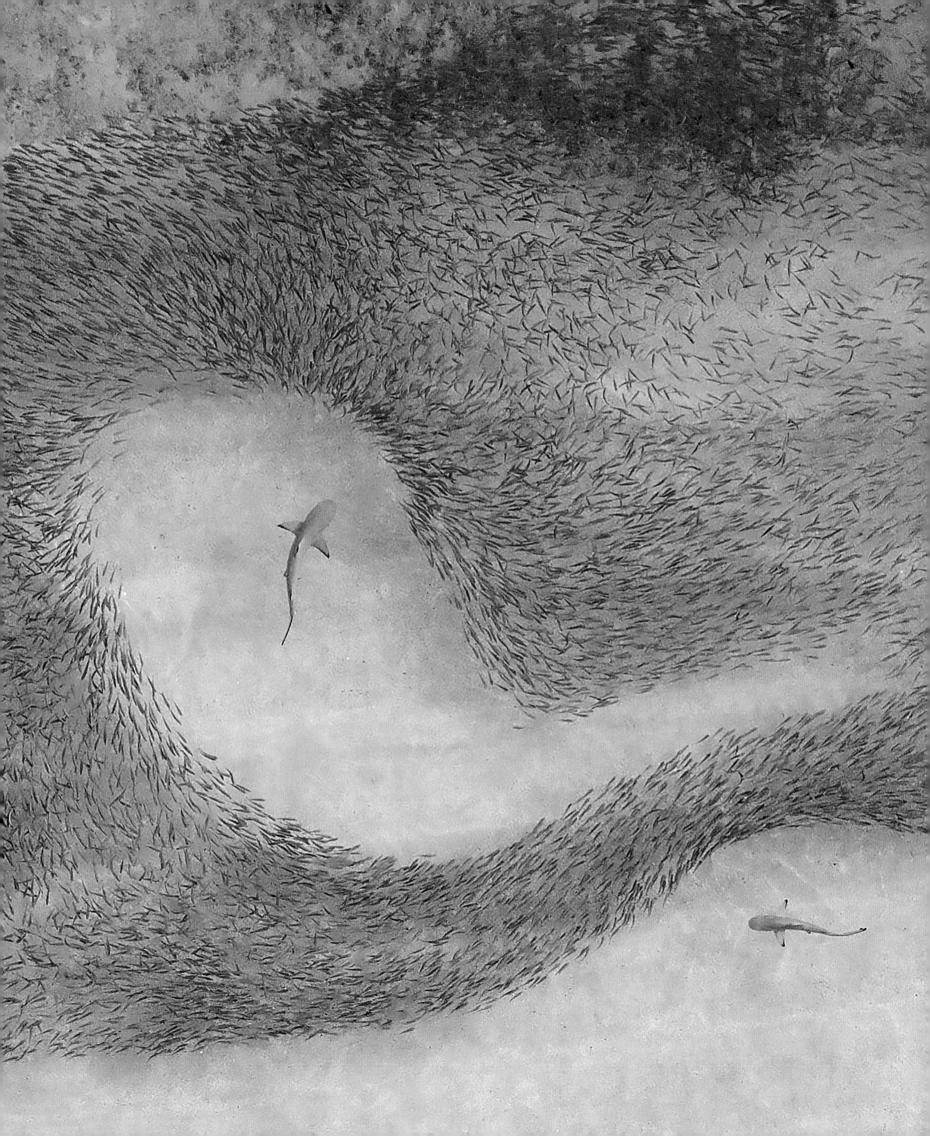

## Slimy blanket

While it sleeps, a steephead parrotfish produces slime from its skin to build up a cocoon around it. This shield takes around an hour to make, and protects the fish from predators and also serves as a barrier to infectious parasites.

## Diversity hotspot

The stunning coral reefs between the Philippines and Papua New Guinea have the highest diversity of marine animals in the world. Known as the Coral Triangle, this region covers six million sq km (2¼ million sq miles) and is also home to 75 per cent of all coral species.

## White-sand islands

Many tiny islands in the western Pacific are surrounded by white beaches made of sand produced by the poop of thousands of coral-eating parrotfish.

## The Philippines

The warm, shallow waters around the Philippines represent the northernmost reach of the Coral Triangle, a region known for its diverse coral reefs and fish species.

## Papua New Guinea

Islands off the coast of this country have some of the richest reefs anywhere on Earth.

AUSTRALASIA

SOLOMON ISLANDS

## Indo-Pacific beauty

The steephead parrotfish is scattered throughout parts of the Indian Ocean to the Pacific islands of Polynesia. This species' showy colours help them to recognize their own kind in crowded, reef-dwelling communities. It also uses its beak to break the rocky coral, digesting its softer flesh and pooping the rocky parts as white sand.

## PARROTFISH HAVE A SET OF **TEETH IN THEIR THROAT** TO GRIND DOWN **ROCKY CORAL**

## North-west Australia

Coral reefs on the narrow continental shelf around this region extend the range of Indo-Pacific fish, such as the steephead parrotfish, into the fringes of the Indian Ocean.

## Head hump

Only males of the steephead parrotfish develop a head hump, but all youngsters have the potential to do so. This is because younger females can change their sex and turn into males.

INDIAN OCEAN

# Steephead parrotfish

Around one-fifth of the world's fish live on tropical coral reefs. Many of these beautiful species, including the steephead parrotfish, are dependent upon coral for their survival, finding shelter in their nooks and crannies. This parrotfish, however, is also known for its unique ability to eat the tough coral using its strong, parrot-like beak.

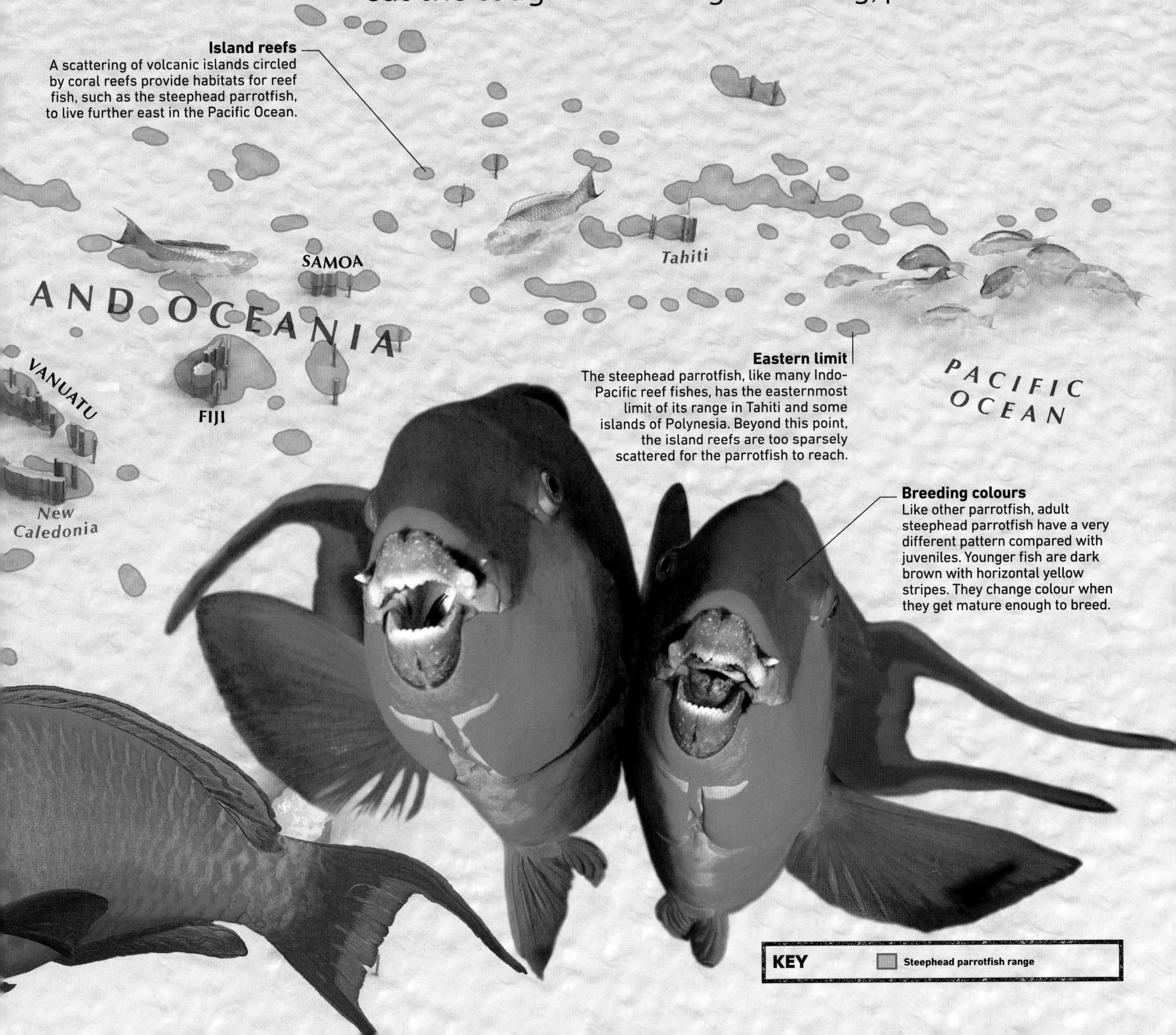

*Hawaii*

**Island reefs**
A scattering of volcanic islands circled by coral reefs provide habitats for reef fish, such as the steephead parrotfish, to live further east in the Pacific Ocean.

SAMOA

*Tahiti*

A N D  O C E A N I A

VANUATU

FIJI

*New Caledonia*

**Eastern limit**
The steephead parrotfish, like many Indo-Pacific reef fishes, has the easternmost limit of its range in Tahiti and some islands of Polynesia. Beyond this point, the island reefs are too sparsely scattered for the parrotfish to reach.

P A C I F I C
O C E A N

**Breeding colours**
Like other parrotfish, adult steephead parrotfish have a very different pattern compared with juveniles. Younger fish are dark brown with horizontal yellow stripes. They change colour when they get mature enough to breed.

**KEY**  Steephead parrotfish range

# RED-BELLIED PIRANHAS "BARK" TO WARN OFF OTHER FISH

**KEY**

■ Red-bellied piranha range

**White waters**
Most red-bellied piranhas live in the cloudier, sediment-heavy "whitewaters" closer to the Amazon's mouth, where the river drains into the Atlantic.

Branco

Rio Negro

Amazon

Madeira

Tapajos

*Amazon Basin*

**Steady waters**
Red-bellied piranhas prefer the lower section of rivers, which are wider, deeper, and move more slowly. They are less likely to be found in the narrower and faster-flowing sections nearer the river's source.

Purus

Guaporé

Andes

**Shoaling**
Piranhas are often feared as blood-thirsty fish that attack big prey in frenzied shoals. But studies have shown that shoaling, as with other fish species, is more a way of protecting themselves from predators. Plenty of Amazon animals, such as giant otters, eat piranhas as prey.

**Carnivorous fish**

Found in rivers, streams, lakes, and flooded forests, the red-bellied piranha is known for its vicious appetite. In reality it usually hunts fish and other small aquatic animals, and avoids anything bigger. Only in the dry season, when pools run low and hungry piranhas are forced together, may piranhas attack bigger land animals that stumble into the waters.

# Red-bellied piranha

The rivers running through the Amazon Basin in northern South America are home to the biggest diversity of freshwater fish in the world, including 38 species of piranha. Among them is the red-bellied piranha – a fish with a fearsome reputation.

**Red bellies**
This species is recognizable for its red belly and silvery body.

**Tocantins**
Many of the rivers that are home to the red-bellied piranha empty into the Amazon. But the Tocantins River empties directly into the Atlantic, so populations of piranhas are cut off from those of the Amazon.

Brazilian Highlands

Sao Francisco

Tocantins

Araguaia

Xingu

**Flowing south**
In the southernmost part of their range, red-bellied piranhas live in the Paraná and Paraguay rivers, which flow through South America's open grasslands and drain into the Atlantic Ocean.

Paraguay

Paraná

Pampas

SOUTH AMERICA

SOME PIRANHAS HAVE A **BITE FORCE** EQUAL TO

**30**

**TIMES THEIR OWN BODY WEIGHT**

**Sharp teeth**
The teeth are arranged in a single row in the upper and lower jaws, and have sharp, blade-like edges for puncturing and cutting through the flesh of animal prey.

## PIRANHA RELATIVES

**Pacu**
A giant relative of the piranhas, the pacu has strong jaws for cracking seeds and nuts that fall into the waters when the Amazon is flooded during the rainy season.

**Neon tetra**
Tetras are tiny relatives of the piranhas that eat small invertebrates. Many, such as the neon tetra, are brightly coloured – making them popular in aquariums.

**Freshwater hatchetfish**
Small piranha relatives called hatchetfishes swim near the surface and prey on insects. Their muscular bodies help them jump from the water to escape danger.

**African tiger fish**
Close cousins of the piranhas live across the Atlantic in African rivers. Some, such as the African tiger fish, are also sharp-toothed meat-eaters.

**Congo tetra**
The brightly coloured Congo tetra lives in Africa. These ancestors of piranha relatives first evolved when South America and Africa were joined.

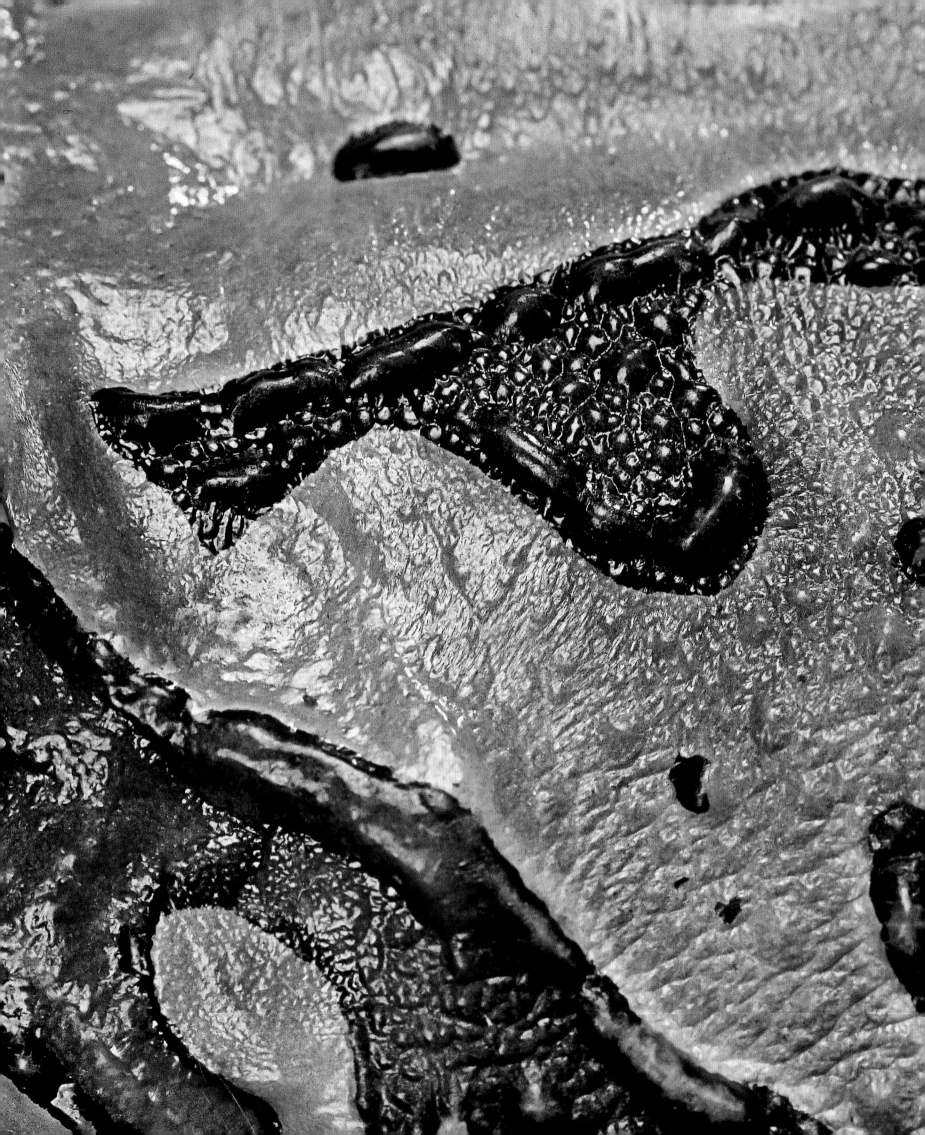

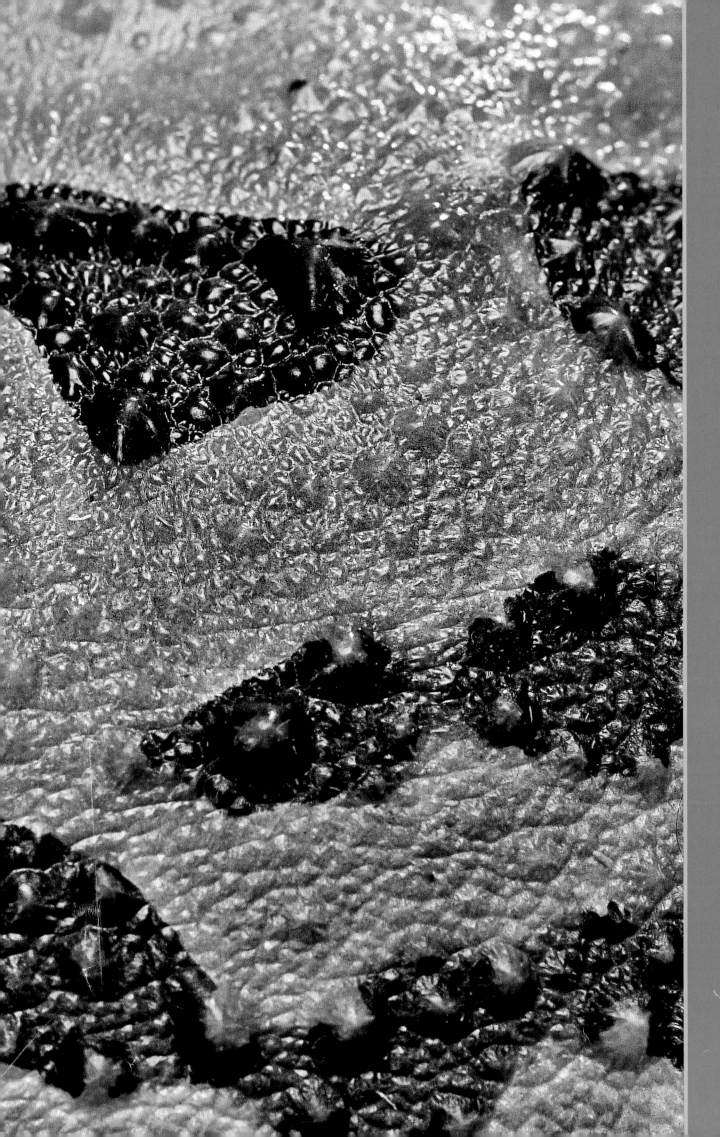

AMPHIBIANS

# Amphibian facts

The first amphibians evolved from fish and moved on to land more than 300 million years ago. Today, most amphibians move between land and water. They are found throughout the world, and most commonly in moist, freshwater habitats like woodlands and rainforests.

## WHAT IS AN AMPHIBIAN?

**Vertebrates**
Like their fish ancestors, all amphibians have an internal skeleton made of bone.

**Cold-blooded**
The body temperature of amphibians fluctuates with that of the air and water around them.

**Lay eggs**
Most amphibians lay soft eggs, but some give birth to live young.

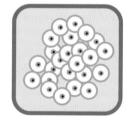

**Aquatic young**
The young hatch and stay for a time as tadpoles in water, eventually turning into amphibious adults.

**Moist skin**
Water passes through an amphibian's thin, moist skin, allowing it to breathe under water.

## AMPHIBIAN TYPES

**ESTIMATED NUMBER OF AMPHIBIAN SPECIES:**  8,250

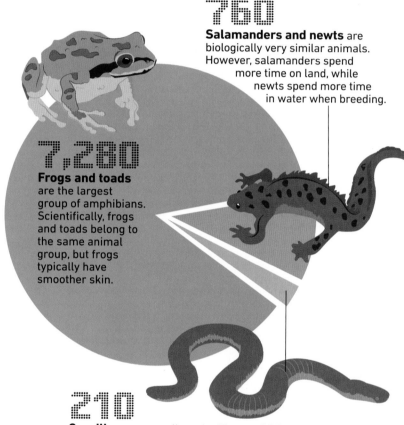

**760**
**Salamanders and newts** are biologically very similar animals. However, salamanders spend more time on land, while newts spend more time in water when breeding.

**7,280**
**Frogs and toads** are the largest group of amphibians. Scientifically, frogs and toads belong to the same animal group, but frogs typically have smoother skin.

**210**
**Caecilians** are small, snake-like amphibians with no limbs and tentacles on their heads. They spend most of their lives underground, eating insects and worms. Some species live in water and have a tail fin for swimming.

## EXTREME HABITATS

These unique amphibians can withstand the toughest conditions, from icy winters to the darkest caves.

**Water-holding frogs** have adapted to harsh Australian deserts. They burrow underground and form a waxy cocoon from layers of skin, which retains moisture necessary for survival.

**Olms** are blind, aquatic salamanders that live in the caves of Slovenia and Croatia. They have excellent smell and hearing, which is helpful when foraging for food, such as snails.

**Crab-eating frogs** are able to tolerate saltier habitats than other amphibians. Native to Southeast Asia, this frog mainly eats insects, but it also preys on crabs, hence its name.

NEARLY **50%** OF ALL **AMPHIBIANS** ARE **THREATENED**, DUE TO WATER **POLLUTION**, HABITAT **DESTRUCTION**, AND THE INTRODUCTION OF **INVASIVE** SPECIES.

# FROG LIFE CYCLE

Most frogs undergo a dramatic physical change from a newborn to an adult through several distinct stages – a process known as metamorphosis.

**2. Tadpoles**
After about 10 days, tadpoles begin to move inside the eggs, before hatching. Over the following weeks, they will develop the ability to swim and eat.

**3. Froglet**
After about nine weeks, the tadpole starts to resemble a frog, with hind and front legs and a pointed head. The long tail will also shorten to a mere stub.

**1. Frogspawn**
After frogs mate, the female lays the eggs in water as a clump called frogspawn. Clear jelly protects the black dot in the middle, which will become the tadpole.

**4. Frog**
At 12 weeks, it is almost a fully formed frog and can leave the water. When it is an adult, it can mate and have young of its own.

# BIGGEST AMPHIBIAN

THE **SOUTH CHINA GIANT SALAMANDER** CAN GROW **1.8m** (6 FT) LONG – ABOUT THE LENGTH OF **FOUR DOMESTIC CATS.**

# SMALLEST AMPHIBIAN

***PAEDOPHRYNE AMAUENSIS*, A FROG FROM PAPUA NEW GUINEA, IS NO BIGGER THAN A FLY, UP TO 7.7 MM (5/16 IN) LONG.**

# ISLAND FROGS

Some frogs live on one island, where the conditons – from the weather and habitat to food – are just right.

**Solomon Island leaf frogs** resemble the colour and shape of leaves on the Solomon Islands in the South Pacific. Curiously, they hatch from eggs as fully developed frogs.

**Gardiner's Seychelles frogs** are one of the tiniest frogs in the world, growing to just 1 cm (3/8 in). Living in the Seychelles, off the eastern edge of Africa, their habitat is threatened by wildfires.

# VENOMOUS AMPHIBIANS

Of all the amphibians, caecilians are probably the most mysterious because they are hard to find in their burrows. However, some experts think these curious creatures, such as the giant caecilian, could have venomous saliva. There are only very few known venomous amphibians, such as Brazil's Greening's frog.

Giant caecilian

# HIGHEST AMPHIBIAN

**BOULENGER'S LAZY TOADS** LIVE **5,270** M (17,290 FT) HIGH, IN **GURUDONGMAR LAKE**, INDIA.

# ONE **GIANT LEAP**

Growing up to 15 cm (6 in), American bullfrogs can leap 20 times their own body length, often pouncing on prey such as insects, fish, and even snakes. They live in freshwater ponds, lakes, and marshes in parts of North America.

The American bullfrog is the largest frog in North America.

**Japanese giant salamander**
This is one of the biggest amphibians – up to 1.4 m (4½ ft) long. It lives in cold mountain streams and gets almost all its oxygen directly through its wrinkled skin.

**Amphiuma**
Only found in North America, this aquatic salamander, with its tiny limbs and eel-like body, has both gills and lungs, but the gills are hidden under flaps of skin.

**Mushroom-tongued salamander**
This tiny salamander is one of nearly 500 species from the American tropics that lack lungs and breathe only through their skin.

**Fire salamander**
This air-breathing salamander from European forests is unusual in giving birth to live young – as aquatic larvae – rather than laying eggs.

**Great crested newt**
Newts are land salamanders that return to water to breed, changing their appearance by developing smoother skin and tail fins.

# Mudpuppy

Salamanders are amphibians shaped like lizards, with long tails and short legs. The mudpuppy is a salamander that lives on river- and lakebeds in North America. They get their unusual name because it was once thought they barked like a dog, but in fact their sound is more like a squeak.

## Lake living
The common mudpuppy is one of eight species of mudpuppies found in the wettest parts of the United States and Canada – mainly in the Great Lakes and the rivers that flow from them. It lurks among the mud and silt, hiding during the day and emerging at night to feed.

**Swamp dweller**
In the warm wet swamps of southern Louisiana, many mudpuppies are yellower than elsewhere in the USA and youngsters often venture out of water into woodland leaf litter.

U N I T E D
S T A T E S

## Organs for breathing
During their lifecycle most amphibians go through a big change called metamorphosis, where their aquatic larva turns into an air-breathing adult. But in some salamanders, such as the mudpuppy, this process is incomplete. The adults keep their gills, allowing them to continue breathing underwater.

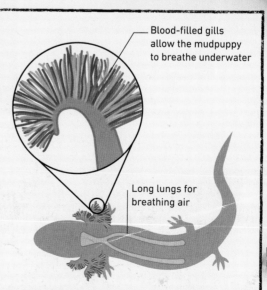

Blood-filled gills allow the mudpuppy to breathe underwater

Long lungs for breathing air

THERE ARE **MORE THAN** **760** **SALAMANDER SPECIES IN THE WORLD**

LIKE ALL OTHER AMPHIBIANS, **MUDPUPPIES** TAKE IN SOME **OXYGEN** DIRECTLY **THROUGH THEIR SKIN**

CANADA

*Hudson Bay*

NORTH AMERICA

**KEY**

☐ Common mudpuppy range

**Great Lakes**
Gills help mudpuppies stay underwater longer than other salamanders. In big lakes they can go as deep as 27 m (88 ft) below the surface to hunt for aquatic invertebrates and the occasional small fish.

*Lake Superior*

*Lake Michigan*

*Lake Huron*

**Finding a mate**
In the northernmost parts of their range, mudpuppies mate in autumn. Females store the male's sperm in their bodies, before laying fertilized eggs the following summer when there is more food.

*Appalachian Mountains*

**Mountain mudpuppy**
In the Appalachian Mountains mudpuppies live in highland streams that run through forests. They stay active even in winter – sometimes swimming beneath ice.

**Coloured skin**
Most mudpuppies are brownish in colour with darker patches that may help with camouflage on riverbeds.

**External gills**
Mudpuppies have external gills – which means they stick out from the body, rather than being hidden under gill flaps. They are bright red because they are filled with blood to pick up oxygen from the surrounding water.

### Mossy frog

The Vietnamese mossy frog lives in the rainforest-covered mountains of northern Vietnam. Its mottled green skin, covered in bumps and ridges, blends in with the wet moss that lines the river banks and caves of the frog's forest habitat. It breeds in water-filled tree holes, laying its eggs above the waterline, safe from predators below.

**Northern range**
The strawberry poison frog reaches as far north as south-eastern Nicaragua. The frogs here may have more purplish-coloured legs and a few black spots on their back.

**Coastal frogs**
The densest populations of frogs occur in the wet lowland rainforest that hugs the Caribbean coasts. Frogs here hop along the ground and occasionally climb into low vegetation.

NICARAGUA

Lake Nicaragua

**KEY**

☐ Strawberry poison frog range

COSTA RICA

## Rainforest frog
Mountains running through Central America keep many different lowland animal species apart on either side. The strawberry poison frog lives in the eastern forest along the Caribbean coast. These frogs are small: adults are only about 2 cm (¾ in) long. Most are bright red with blue or black legs – but in some places colours vary.

**Calling out**
Strawberry frogs live on plants near to the forest floor. The males use their low, buzzing call to defend their tiny territories and attract females.

**Blue jeans**
Most strawberry poison frogs have red bodies and blue legs, earning them the nickname "blue jeans" frogs. In the south of their range some mainland frogs are greyish or yellow.

## Plant pool
Strawberry poison frogs are careful parents. They lay their eggs on forest leaves. When they hatch, the tadpoles are carried on the mother's back to a pool of water in a bromeliad plant, where they turn into frogs.

## Colour varieties
The strawberry poison frog comes in more than 100 different coloured varieties called morphs. Most of these varieties occur on tiny islands off the Central American coast, where frogs are cut off from those on the mainland. They have different colours because their populations have been separated for thousands of years and have evolved to look different.

**Colour morphs of the strawberry poison frog**

# Strawberry poison frog

Most amphibians rely on poisons to defend themselves. Glands in their skin ooze chemicals that can be irritating or even deadly. The strawberry poison frog from Central America excels at defending itself in this way – and warns off enemies with its bright colours.

**Island frogs**
The tiny islands of Bocas del Toro off the Caribbean coast of Panama are home to many different colours of strawberry poison frogs (see panel below).

PANAMA

**Poison skin**
The skin is moistened by secretions from two types of gland: one produces mucus and makes it slimy, the other oozes poison that tastes repulsive to predators.

# Common toad

Amphibians need moisture to survive, but some are tolerant of a range of different habitats. The common toad, one of more than 600 toad species across the world, is the most widespread in Europe. It lives equally well in forests, alpine meadows, and dry sand dunes.

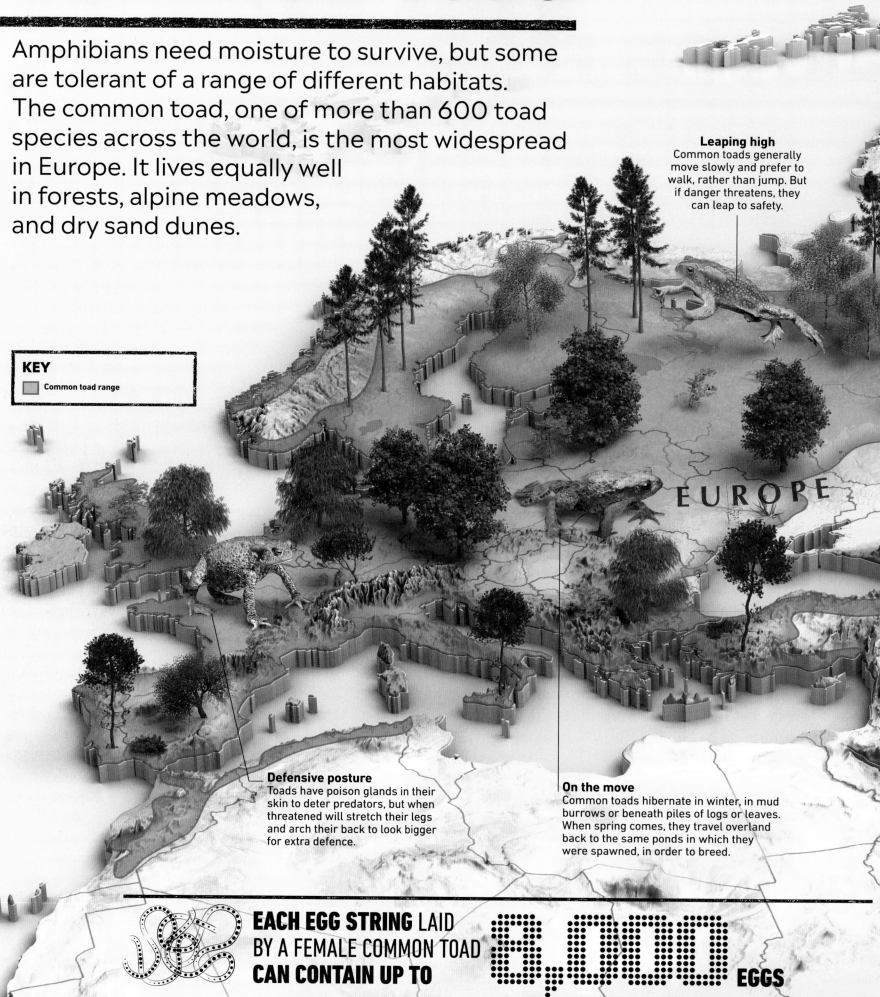

**KEY**

Common toad range

EUROPE

**Leaping high**
Common toads generally move slowly and prefer to walk, rather than jump. But if danger threatens, they can leap to safety.

**Defensive posture**
Toads have poison glands in their skin to deter predators, but when threatened will stretch their legs and arch their back to look bigger for extra defence.

**On the move**
Common toads hibernate in winter, in mud burrows or beneath piles of logs or leaves. When spring comes, they travel overland back to the same ponds in which they were spawned, in order to breed.

**EACH EGG STRING** LAID BY A FEMALE COMMON TOAD **CAN CONTAIN UP TO** 6,000 EGGS

## Breeding pools
Like most amphibians, toads lay their eggs in pools of water. The female common toad lays her eggs in two long strings, each up to 5 m (16 ft) long. The eggs will hatch into aquatic larvae, or tadpoles.

## Mass migration
Each springtime large numbers of common toads emerge from hibernation and travel to their breeding pools. In some places, special toad-crossing tunnels have been built to help them cross roads safely.

## Mating toads
When mating in ponds, the male toad grabs the larger female around the waist just behind her front legs and then fertilizes the strings of eggs as they are released into the water.

ASIA

## Temperate belt
The common toad is found throughout much of Europe – in the temperate belt south of the cold polar regions and north of hotter Africa and Asia. It lives most of its life away from water, hiding in damp, shady places, returning to the water only to breed.

## Bulging eyes
The large eyes of a common toad give it good night vision. Common toads are most active at night, using the cover of darkness to hunt for prey.

## Tongue attack
The toad catches invertebrate prey, such as slugs, snails, and spiders, with a long sticky-tipped tongue that shoots out of its mouth at lightning speed.

REPTILES

# Reptile facts

Scaly and cold-blooded, reptiles first appeared around 310 million years ago and were the first backboned animals that could live entirely on land. From desert snakes to migrating sea turtles, reptiles today are scattered throughout the world, except the very coldest habitats.

## WHAT IS A REPTILE?

**Vertebrates**
From slithery snakes to giant tortoises, all reptiles are supported by a bony skeleton.

**Cold-blooded**
The body temperature of all reptiles changes depending on their environment.

**Lay eggs**
Most reptiles, from crocodiles to lizards, lay soft, leathery, and waterproof eggs.

**Live young**
Some snakes and lizards do not lay eggs like most other reptiles, but instead give birth to live young.

**Scaly skin**
Reptilian skin is covered in protective scales, or in some cases, horny plates.

## REPTILE TYPES

**ESTIMATED NUMBER OF REPTILE SPECIES:** 11,340

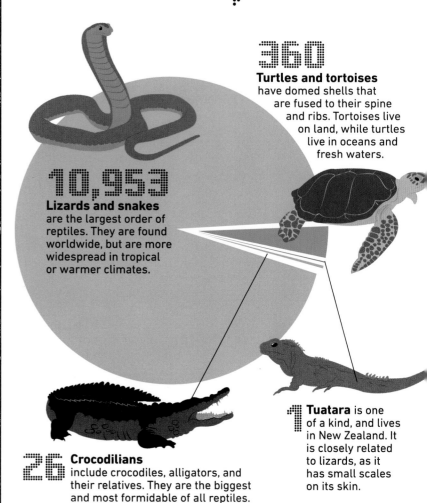

**360**
**Turtles and tortoises** have domed shells that are fused to their spine and ribs. Tortoises live on land, while turtles live in oceans and fresh waters.

**10,953**
**Lizards and snakes** are the largest order of reptiles. They are found worldwide, but are more widespread in tropical or warmer climates.

**26 Crocodilians** include crocodiles, alligators, and their relatives. They are the biggest and most formidable of all reptiles. They spend most of their time in water, although some hunt on land.

**1 Tuatara** is one of a kind, and lives in New Zealand. It is closely related to lizards, as it has small scales on its skin.

## EXTREME HABITATS
From the freezing Arctic to underground burrows in the desert, some reptiles survive and thrive in the most incredible ways.

**Common European adders** are the only snake species found within the Arctic Circle. Its huge range also extends from temperate woodlands to the European Alps 3,000 m (9,840 ft) high.

**Gopher tortoises** survive the intense heat and cold of the American Mojave Desert by burrowing underground with their sharp claws. They spend up to 95 per cent of their lives in these burrows.

**Sea snakes** are the best-adapted reptile for life in water. All true sea snakes give birth to live young, without ever coming ashore to lay eggs. They live mainly in tropical oceans.

## LONGEST MIGRATION

**LEATHERBACK TURTLES** CAN TRAVEL **20,500** KM (12,750 MILES) FROM THEIR **INDONESIAN** BREEDING GROUND TO FEED OFF THE PACIFIC COAST OF **THE USA.**

# BIGGEST GATHERING

EACH **SPRING** INSIDE THE SNAKE DENS OF NARCISSE, **MANITOBA, CANADA,** **75,000** **RED-SIDED GARTER SNAKES** CONGREGATE IN A MATING FRENZY, WITH UP TO **100 MALES** VYING FOR **EVERY FEMALE.**

# SMALLEST REPTILE

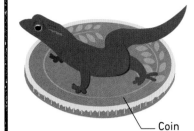

— Coin

THE **VIRGIN ISLANDS DWARF SPHAERO** IS ONLY **1.6** CM (⅝ IN) LONG.

# OLDEST REPTILE

BORN IN **1832**, THE **OLDEST-LIVING** LAND ANIMAL IS A **SEYCHELLES GIANT TORTOISE** CALLED **JONATHAN**.

# LONGEST REPTILE

THE **RETICULATED PYTHON** OF SOUTHEAST ASIA HAS SET THE RECORD-BREAKING LENGTH OF **10** M (33 FT).

# FASTEST REPTILE

In a reptilian race between the fastest snake and swiftest lizard, the lizard would easily cross the finish line first.

**FASTEST SNAKE:** SIDEWINDER AT **28 KM/H** (18 MPH)

**FASTEST LIZARD:** BEARDED DRAGON AT **40 KM/H** (25 MPH)

# SNAKE MOTION

A snake can move in four main ways. Some species can switch between styles of moving, depending on the surface.

**Straight**
Scales along a snake's belly provide traction on the ground for it to propel itself in a line, using the muscles around its long ribcage.

Snake moves diagonally

**Sidewinding**
In open spaces such as sandy deserts, some snakes fling their head sideways through the air, with the rest of the body following.

Tail is pressed to the ground as snake bunches up

Snake launches, then bunches up again

**Concertina**
To get a good grip on a smooth surface, a snake can bunch up before pulling its back end up and launching itself forward.

Rock

Snake adopts an S shape

**Serpentine**
This common style involves a snake pushing itself off a bump on a surface or an object, and continuing forwards in a wavy motion.

# HIGHEST-LIVING REPTILE

THE **RED TAIL TOAD-HEADED LIZARD** HAS BEEN SEEN AT **5,300** M (17,390 FT). IT LIVES IN THE QIANGTANG PLATEAU IN NORTHERN TIBET.

# SMART REPTILE

The mugger crocodile in India has been observed using sticks to lure birds, such as egrets or herons, who may be looking to build a nest. It waits motionless and partially submerged, then snaps up its unsuspecting prey when it is close enough.

## KEY

- ☐ Volcán Wolf giant tortoise
- ☐ Fernandina giant tortoise
- ☐ Volcán Alcedo giant tortoise
- ☐ Santiago giant tortoise
- ☐ Santa Cruz giant tortoise
- ☐ San Cristóbal giant tortoise
- ☐ Española giant tortoise

### ANIMALS IN DANGER

Of the 14 species of Galápagos giant tortoise listed by the IUCN, six are regarded as critically endangered, three as endangered, two as extinct, and the rest as vulnerable. Hunting and habitat destruction have been threats in the past, but now conservation measures are slowly making progress.

*Isla Pinta*

*Isla Marchena*

PACIFIC OCEAN

**Santiago giant tortoise**
Giant tortoises on Santiago have been hunted extensively in the past, but protection is now helping to restore the species. Their shells are intermediate, between dome-shaped and saddleback-shaped.

*Isla Santiago*

**Volcán Wolf giant tortoise**
Volcán Wolf, the highest volcano in the Galápagos, on the island of Isabela, is home to a species of giant tortoises that have either domed shells or saddleback shells, like the one shown here.

**Volcán Alcedo giant tortoise**
The different habitats on Isabela has meant that different species of giant tortoise have evolved there. Those on the volcano of Alcedo have a black, domed shell.

*Isla Pinzón*

*Isla Fernandina*

*Isla Isabela*

**Fernandina giant tortoise**
For more than 100 years, the saddleback-shelled tortoises from the island of Fernandina were thought to be extinct, until a century-old female was discovered in 2019, raising hopes that others have survived too.

**Horny beak**
Tortoises lack teeth, but instead have a sharp-edged beak that is used to crop vegetation – mostly in the form of grass, shrubs, cactuses, and the occasional fruit.

**Bony shell**
Like other tortoises, giant tortoises have a hard, protective shell made from bony plates that are fused to the reptile's backbone and ribs.

**Santa Cruz giant tortoise**

# THE **ESTIMATED** LIFESPAN OF A GALÁPAGOS **GIANT TORTOISE** IS **170 YEARS**

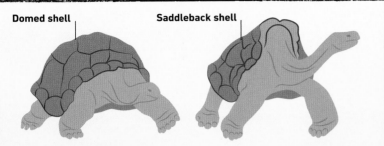

**Domed shell**  **Saddleback shell**

### Shell shape and diet

On wetter islands with plenty of ground plants to graze, the shells of Galápagos giant tortoises are dome-shaped. But on drier islands, tortoises have evolved raised shells – called saddlebacks – and long necks. This helps them reach tall cactuses that grow higher from the ground.

### Lonesome George

In 1971, scientists found the only surviving Pinta Island giant tortoise. The rest of its kind had died out, due to the overgrazing by goats introduced to the island. Named Lonesome George, this tortoise became a symbol of conservation, living out his life in captivity. He died in 2012.

*Isla Santa Cruz*

### San Cristóbal giant tortoise

Animals introduced to this island, such as dogs and donkeys, drove San Cristóbal tortoises almost to extinction, but better control measures and captive breeding are helping to save the species.

*Isla San Cristóbal*

*Isla Santa Fe*

### Santa Cruz giant tortoise

The dome-shelled giant tortoises of Santa Cruz live in separate populations on this island, and studies suggest that they might be different species.

### Island giants

The Galápagos Islands erupted from the ocean more than three million years ago. Tortoises landed on their shores after floating across the waters from South America. With no natural predators, they evolved into giants and, as they adapted to the different conditions and food sources on each island, into separate species. Seven of these are shown on this map.

### Española giant tortoise

On one of the oldest and most barren of the Galápagos Islands, Española tortoises have especially high-saddled shells to help them reach up to nibble on the scarce food growing here, such as cactuses.

*Isla Española*

*Galápagos Islands*

*Isla Santa Maria*

# Galápagos giant tortoises

Tortoises are slow-moving reptiles with a heavy, protective shell. Some of the biggest tortoises on Earth live on the rugged, volcanic Galápagos Islands far out in the Pacific Ocean. Each island is home to its own species.

**KEY**

☐ Alligators and caimans
☐ Crocodiles
☐ Gharials

This map shows the combined ranges
of all the species in each group.

**American
alligator**
The American
alligator is the
northernmost
crocodilian in the
Americas. During
the coolest months,
it basks in the sun
to keep warm.

## Who lives where?

The crocodiles are the largest group
and the most wide ranging – 16
species live in either Africa, Asia,
or the Americas. Alligators and
caimans, of which there are
eight species in total, only
occur in the Americas and
China. Two species
of gharials live
in Southeast Asia.

AFRICA

**Nile crocodile**
The most widespread crocodilian
on the African continent, the Nile
crocodile is also its biggest
freshwater predator. Adults
prey on antelope coming
to drink at waterholes.

**Spectacled caiman**
Caimans, found in tropical
America, are smaller relatives
of alligators. The spectacled
caiman is one of the most
common, found in many
slow-moving rivers,
ponds, and lakes
across its range.

SOUTH
AMERICA

**Crocodile teeth**
Crocodilians are the only
reptiles that grow teeth
from sockets in the
jaws – more like those
of mammals. Teeth are
replaced as they wear
down or fall out.

**Boy or girl?**
Crocodilian eggs get incubated
in a nest, wrapped in warm soil
or vegetation, before hatching
like this little Nile crocodile.
There can be up to 80 eggs
in a nest, and the sex of each
depends on its temperature.
The warmer eggs turn male
and the cooler ones female.

**Saltwater
crocodile**

EUROPE

### Different head shapes

The three types of crocodilians differ mainly in the shapes of their snouts: alligators and caimans typically have broader snouts than crocodiles, while the fish-eating gharials have the slenderest snouts of all, ending in a bulb-like growth. Many crocodiles show exposed teeth in the lower jaw, even with their jaws closed.

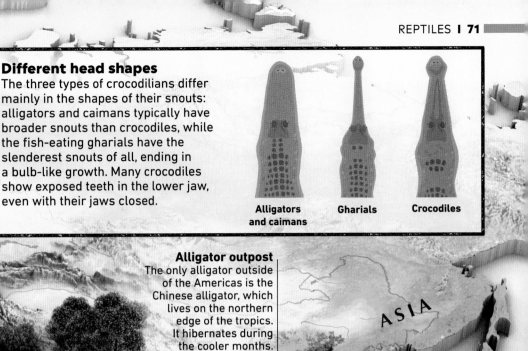

Alligators and caimans   Gharials   Crocodiles

### Alligator outpost

The only alligator outside of the Americas is the Chinese alligator, which lives on the northern edge of the tropics. It hibernates during the cooler months.

ASIA

### Mugger crocodile

The mugger lives in the shallows of wetlands on the Indian subcontinent. It burrows underground to escape the fiercest heat of the sun.

### Saltwater crocodile

The world's largest crocodilian is also the most salt-tolerant. "Salties" often swim in coastal ocean waters, and have spread across a wide range of islands in Asia and Australasia and Oceania.

### Gharial

The gharial from mainland Asia, and the false gharial from islands further south, spend more time in water than other crocodilians. They specialize in hunting for fish and, sometimes, frogs.

# Crocodilians

The world's biggest reptiles live wherever it is warm enough for them to hunt and raise a family – by rivers and lakes in tropical regions on both sides of the equator. They are divided into three groups: alligators and caimans, crocodiles, and gharials.

AUSTRALIA

**110** THE **NUMBER OF TEETH** OF A **GHARIAL – MORE** THAN ANY OTHER CROCODILIAN

THERE ARE **FEWER THAN 80** ADULT **CHINESE ALLIGATORS** LEFT IN THE WILD

# Chameleons

Strange-looking, slow-moving lizards with conical eyes and grasping tails, chameleons live in the tropics of Africa and southern Asia. Over half of the 200 chameleon species are found on the island of Madagascar and nowhere else. The island is home to the biggest and smallest of them all.

**Madagascan giant chameleon**
The world's biggest species of chameleon – growing nearly 70 cm (27½ in) long – is one of the most widespread in Madagascar. It survives equally well in dry and wet forests, all over the island.

**Labord's chameleon**
In the dry west of Madagascar, Labord's chameleon lives just five months before laying eggs during brief rains, and then dies. No other land vertebrate has such a short life.

**Catching prey**
Like all chameleons, the Madagascan giant chameleon catches insects and other prey by shooting out its long projectile tongue, which has a sticky end to trap the target.

MADAGASCAR

**Elongate leaf chameleon**
One of many species of short-tailed leaf chameleons, this one lives in the branches of low bushes, and mimics a dead leaf to hide from predators.

## Madagascar chameleons

Almost all chameleons live in forests. Some climb the trees while others live on the ground. This map shows five of the chameleon species that live on Madagascar. The island is drier in the west and wetter in the east, and it is in the rich rainforests of eastern Madagascar that most species occur, but many are now threatened by deforestation.

A CHAMELEON'S **TONGUE** CAN EXTEND **TWICE THE LENGTH** OF ITS **BODY**

**Panther chameleon**
Male panther chameleons vary a great deal in colour depending on where they live. Some are red, green, and yellow, others are turquoise-green or greyish. Most females are pinkish-brown.

## Chameleon colours
Chameleons have a famous ability to change colour, usually according to their mood. A male panther chameleon switches to an especially bright pattern when showing off to potential mates or competing males. The colour change comes from tiny crystals in the skin that reflect light in different ways.

**Parson's chameleon**
In some chameleons, such as the Parson's chameleon, the males have prominent horns on their nose, which they use in "jousting" contests when defending territory.

**Body shape**
A chameleon's body has flat sides, making its high-arched back look like a crest running from head to tail. Green or brown colours help to hide chameleons among leaves.

**Feet for gripping**
The five toes of a chameleon foot are fused together into two mitten-like pads. This unique arrangement helps them hold on tightly to any branch.

**Parson's chameleon**

**Prehensile tail**
Chameleons are among the very few lizards with completely prehensile tails. This means they can use their tail like a fifth limb to grip branches as they climb through trees.

## Mini chameleon
The world's smallest chameleon, known only by its scientific name of *Brookesia micra*, is also one of the smallest reptiles in the world. It can grow to just 3 cm (1⅛ in) long, tail included, and spends its life among leaf litter. It was discovered on the tiny islet of Nosy Hara off the north coast of Madagascar.

## Armoured lizard
The dragon-like armadillo girdled lizard is covered by protective spiny plates – except on its underside. To shield its soft belly from predator attacks, it grabs hold of its tail and curls up in a ball, like an armadillo (see p.109). This lizard lives in large family groups inside rock crevices in South Africa's western deserts.

# Green anaconda

All snakes prey on other animals, but the biggest kill by constriction, rather than venom. The green anaconda, at home in South America, is the heaviest of all constrictors, and can tackle animals the size of small deer.

**River snake**
More than 1,000 rivers run through the Amazon Basin, making it the perfect habitat for the green anaconda, which can swim faster than it crawls on land.

Orinoco

Amazon

Amazon

SOUTH AMERICA

Amazon Basin

**Big meal**
Loosely connected jaw bones and a stretchy body help an anaconda swallow prey whole. Large prey, such as deer or caimans, can take weeks to digest.

Andes

ANACONDAS **GIVE BIRTH** TO UP TO

**50**

**YOUNG AT A TIME**

**KEY**
■ Green anaconda range

**Squeezed prey**
Constrictors such as anacondas kill not by crushing, but by suffocation. The snake squeezes tighter each time its victim exhales, so breathing becomes impossible, and the heart stops.

**Wetland giant**
The green anaconda grows so heavy that adult snakes tend to stick to rivers and wetlands, where their bodies are supported by water. The river-filled Amazon Basin merges with grasslands in the south, where much of the land is flooded during the rainy season, making a large part of South America prime anaconda habitat.

**Top vision**
The eyes of a green anaconda are set higher on the head than those of many other snakes. This helps it keep watch at the water's surface, while its body is submerged.

**Scaly skin**
As it grows, the anaconda needs to shed its scaly skin several times a year, but the pattern of black oval spots on a muddy green background doesn't change.

Pantanal

**Chunky waist**
At its thickest, an anaconda's body can have a diameter of up to 30 cm (12 in).

**Reticulated python**
The green anaconda is the heaviest, but the longest snake is likely to be the reticulated python from Southeast Asia, with recorded lengths of more than 7 m (23 ft).

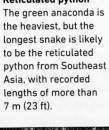

**African rock python**
The biggest snake in Africa, growing to 6 m (20 ft) long, the African rock python has the strength to prey on large crocodiles.

**Burmese python**
Weighing around 180 kg (400 lb), the Burmese python from Southeast Asia is the heaviest recorded snake after the green anaconda.

**Indian rock python**
Only slightly smaller than the Burmese and African rock pythons, this snake swims well and is common in wetlands and forests of India and Sri Lanka.

**Amethystine python**
Australia's largest snake hunts possums and wallabies, and sometimes slides into human homes. It is also widespread in New Guinea and nearby islands.

## NORTH AMERICA

**Western diamondback rattlesnake**
One of the largest venomous snakes found in North America, this rattlesnake hunts desert rodents, but is also responsible for many human injuries in the US.

## Deadly snakes
The warm tropics are home to the greatest number of snake species. The most dangerous venomous types belong to two groups: vipers, with large, hinged fangs, and elapids, with shorter fangs that are always raised. This map shows seven of the world's deadliest snakes.

**Common lancehead**
A relative of the rattlesnakes, the common lancehead moves about at night, and is one of the most dangerous vipers found in the tropical forests of South America.

## SOUTH AMERICA

## AFRICA

**Fangs**
Rattlesnakes are vipers, and have some of the biggest fangs of any snake. The largest rattlesnakes can have fangs more than 5 cm (2 in) long.

**Warning rattle**
The tail tip rattle is made up of special scales that produce a warning sound when shaken if predators come too close.

**Black mamba**
Named for the black lining of its mouth, this elapid is one of the longest and fastest of the venomous snakes in Africa and quickly inflicts multiple dangerous bites.

Western diamondback rattlesnake

## Snake venom
Venom is a poisonous fluid that flows from glands in the snake's upper jaw. When the snake bites, a muscle squeezes venom out through the fangs. Viper fangs reach further forwards than those of elapids.

**Elapid**
Elapids have small, fixed fangs at the back of the jaw

**Viper**
Viper fangs swing forwards as the jaw opens

### KEY
- Western diamondback rattlesnake
- Common lancehead
- Black mamba
- Saw-scaled viper
- Indian cobra
- Many-banded krait
- Tiger snake

# Venomous snakes

There are around 3,850 species of snakes around the world, and about 20 per cent of these are venomous. They use their venom to kill their prey – but some also strike in self-defence and, when they do so, some species can be dangerous to humans, such as the ones shown here.

Arabian Peninsula

ASIA

INDIA

AUSTRALIA

**Saw-scaled viper**
With a dangerous bite, and often found living close to humans, this snake is probably responsible for more human deaths than any other. Similar saw-scaled vipers occur elsewhere on the Arabian Peninsula and in parts of Africa.

**Indian cobra**
The Indian cobra is an elapid that warns anyone approaching that it will strike in self-defence. It extends ribs close to its neck to produce a flat hood, while rising up to appear bigger.

**Many-banded krait**
Kraits are boldly patterned elapid snakes found across Asia. Living near water, the many-banded krait hides during the day and hunts at night, preying on fish. If surprised, it uses its deadly bite in self-defence.

**Tiger snake**
The tiger snake is one of many highly venomous elapid snakes found in Australia. Individuals vary in colour and not all have the stripes that give the species its name.

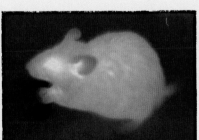

**Hunting by heat**
Vipers have an extra sense that helps them locate prey. Heat-sensitive pits on their head allow them to "see" the body heat of warm-blooded animals, in the same way that the mouse shows up against a cold background in this thermal image.

ABOUT **200** **SNAKE SPECIES** HAVE **VENOM** THAT IS HARMFUL TO **HUMANS**

AROUND **138,000** **PEOPLE DIE** FROM A SNAKE **BITE** EVERY **YEAR**

# BIRDS

# Bird facts

Evolving from two-legged dinosaurs, the first birds took flight about 140 million years ago. Today, birds are found on every continent and in a diverse range of habitats, from grasslands to deserts. Many birds migrate incredibly long distances, to breed or find food.

## WHAT IS A BIRD?

**Vertebrates**
Birds have thin and lightweight, yet strong, internal skeletons made of bone.

**Warm-blooded**
From humid rainforests to chilly mountaintops, birds generate and maintain a stable body temperature.

**Lay eggs**
Birds breed by laying hard eggs, which chicks crack open when ready to hatch.

**Most fly**
Using their wings, most birds can take to the skies, however some birds are flightless.

**Feathered**
Feathers are important for retaining body heat and helping birds to fly.

## BIRD TYPES

**ESTIMATED NUMBER OF BIRD SPECIES:** 11,500

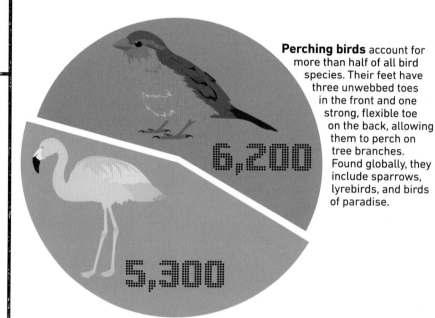

**Perching birds** account for more than half of all bird species. Their feet have three unwebbed toes in the front and one strong, flexible toe on the back, allowing them to perch on tree branches. Found globally, they include sparrows, lyrebirds, and birds of paradise.

6,200

5,300

**Non-perching birds** account for all other species. They include a wide range of birds located across the world including parrots, owls, flamingos, and birds of prey, as well as flightless birds, such as ostriches, emus, and penguins.

**COLOMBIA** HAS OVER 1,850 BIRD SPECIES – **MORE THAN ANY OTHER COUNTRY** IN THE WORLD.

## HIBERNATING BIRD

**The common poorwill,** seen here on a roof, is the only bird species known to hibernate. Its diet of insects rapidly declines during winter, so it goes into a state of hibernation for weeks or even months. This bird is found in the grassy areas of North America.

## LONGEST MIGRATION

**ARCTIC TERNS** CAN FLY AN AMAZING 96,000 KM (59,650 MILES) FROM THEIR BREEDING GROUND IN THE **NORTH ATLANTIC** TO **ANTARCTICA** AND BACK AGAIN.

## BIGGEST GATHERING

Flocks of more than 1.5 billion red-billed quelea have been witnessed flying over the African savanna. In such great numbers, this small bird is a constant threat to crop farmers. In fact, it is such a pest, it is often called the "feathered locust".

# BILL SHAPES

Over millions of years, birds have evolved many different bill shapes. Here are five of them, each designed to help the bird eat or catch its prey.

### Seed-eater
Birds such as crossbills have strong bills for eating seeds. The crossbill can extract seeds from pine cones with its overlapping bill.

### Water-sifter
Flamingos have long, wide bills that they sweep from side to side in shallow waters, sifting out animals to eat.

### Nectar-gatherer
The pointed bills are designed for precision. Sunbirds' bills also curve downwards, which is ideal for extracting flower nectar.

### Mud probe
Birds with long, sensitive bills can explore soft mud in search of prey. The snipe looks for snails and small crustaceans.

### Butchery tool
This hooked bill, as seen on a golden eagle, is perfect for stripping meat from the bones of fish, birds, or mammals.

---

## THE **LARGEST FLYING BIRD** IS THE **WANDERING ALBATROSS,** WITH A WINGSPAN OF **3.6** M (12 FT).

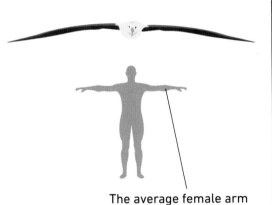

The average female arm span is about 1.6 m (5.2 ft).

## BIGGEST BIRD AND EGGS

THE OSTRICH, A FLIGHTLESS BIRD FROM SUB-SAHARAN AFRICA, IS THE WORLD'S TALLEST BIRD.

IT ALSO BEARS THE LARGEST EGGS, UP TO **15** CM (6 IN) LONG – NEARLY THREE TIMES LONGER THAN A HEN'S EGG.

## SMALLEST BIRD

THE **BEE HUMMINGBIRD** GROWS TO JUST **6** CM (2.4 IN). THIS TINY BIRD IS NATIVE TO **CUBA.**

---

## FASTEST BIRD

Found throughout the world, peregrine falcons are formidable hunters. They swoop in on prey, such as other birds and bats, at a record-breaking speed.

SWOOPING SPEED = **320 KM/H** (200 MPH)

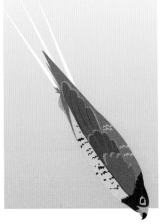

RÜPPELL'S VULTURE

**10,670 M (35,000 FT)**

## HIGHEST-FLYING BIRD

**RÜPPELL'S VULTURE** CAN REACH AN ALTITUDE OF **11,280** M (37,000 FT), HIGHER THAN THE CRUISING ALTITUDE OF AN AEROPLANE.

## BIGGEST NEST

**SOCIABLE WEAVERS** MAKE AND MAINTAIN NESTS THAT CAN HOUSE UP TO **500** BIRDS.

## SMART BIRD

Found in the remote Pacific islands after which it is named, the New Caledonian crow can manipulate and use twigs to dig out prey, such as grubs, from trees. These intelligent forest-dwelling birds are the first to be observed making and using tools in this way.

**Rheas**
Found on the South American pampas, rheas resemble ostriches, but are smaller, with three-toed feet. Both sexes have brown plumage.

**Tinamous**
These are chicken-sized birds from tropical American grassland and forest. They are the only close ostrich relatives that can take to the air, but they are weak fliers.

**Cassowaries**
The largest flightless birds from dense rainforest are found in tropical New Guinea and northeastern Australia. They have blue skin on the head and neck.

**Emu**
Most closely related to the cassowaries, the emu lives on open grassland and deserts of Australia. Like the ostrich, it is adapted to dry conditions.

**Kiwis**
From the forests of New Zealand, the five species of kiwi are the smallest ostrich relatives and have long bills to probe the ground for prey.

## Out in the open

Ostriches are at home on open countryside from desert to savanna, where they live in groups and wander long distances in search of food and water. Food is scarce, so ostriches will eat whatever they can find – roots, seeds, insects, and even small reptiles and mammals.

**Male ostrich**
Male common ostriches have back plumage with white wings and tail and skin. The females are brownish all over.

**Common ostrich**
In northern Africa the common ostrich lives mainly in the dry grassland Sahel region, but may wander right to the edge of the Sahara Desert.

S a h a r a

S a h e l

Common ostrich

**Built to run**
The long-legged ostrich is the only bird with just two toes. This reduces the area of each foot in contact with the ground, increasing speed.

**KEY**
Common ostrich
Somali ostrich

**ANIMALS IN DANGER**
Somali ostrich
IUCN status: vulnerable
Population estimate: unknown

# Ostriches

A bird that can't fly, and roams where there is very little cover, has to run fast to escape predators. The flightless ostrich does just that. As well as being the world's biggest bird it is the fastest animal on two legs. There are two species and both live in open habitats in Africa.

**Ostrich chicks**
All female ostriches in the group lay their eggs in a communal nest, so adults may end up guarding large crèches of chicks.

Great Rift Valley

Congo Basin

AFRICA

**Somali ostrich**
This species lives in the eastern horn of Africa – in Somalia, Ethiopia, and Kenya. Males have a grey head, neck, legs, and feet, and a deeper black plumage than the common ostrich.

**Masai region**
In the Masai region of east Africa common ostriches have a reddish-tinge to their neck but are more closely related to the grey-necked ostriches further south.

**Rift Valley**
The two species of ostrich are separated by the Great Rift Valley (pictured below). On the eastern side the Somali ostrich has split away from common ostriches and evolved into a separate species.

**Desert dweller**
In the southernmost part of their range, common ostriches live in hot, dry desert.

Kalahari Desert

Namib Desert

**MALE OSTRICHES STAND UP TO 2.7 M (9 FT) TALL**

**AT TOP SPEED** AN OSTRICH CAN RUN ABOUT 70 KM/H (43 MPH) – THAT'S **FASTER THAN A RACEHORSE**

## Changing colours

Each year, thousands of Caribbean flamingos are born in one of the world's largest flamingo colonies, Mexico's Ría Lagartos Biosphere Reserve. The chicks' grey feathers turn pink when they eat shrimp and other invertebrates containing a dye. This bird's population is rising, from the Caribbean to South America.

**KEY**
- Breeding site
- Swimming range

SOUTHERN OCEAN

Weddell Sea

Ronne Ice Shelf

ANTARCTICA

South Pole

Ross Ice Shelf

Ross Sea

**Sleek swimmer**
The streamlined body of a penguin is superbly adapted for swimming. Underwater, these birds flap their paddle-like wings for propulsion.

**Contact call**
The call of an emperor penguin can be heard more than 1 km (half a mile) away. Each bird recognizes the call of its mate, which helps them to locate one another in the crowded colony.

**Feeding time**
Males feed their chick with a special curd produced from their food-pipe, until the mother arrives with fish and krill caught at sea.

**Standing tall**
Penguins stand very upright because their feet are set far back on the body. The emperor is the tallest of all – up to 1.3 m (4¼ ft).

**Breeding site**
At colonies around the coast, emperors gather to find a mate. The female lays a single egg then returns to the sea, leaving the male to incubate the egg alone.

## Polar penguin

Emperor penguins feed in the icy waters of the Southern Ocean around Antarctica. They can dive deeper than any other seabird to catch fish and krill. Each year, emperors gather in their thousands at breeding sites around the coast to mate and raise their single chicks.

# Emperor penguin

The life of the world's biggest penguin is a story of surviving extremes. It is one of the very few animals to live and breed on the Antarctic continent – the coldest place on Earth. Emperor penguins raise their chicks in the dark, bitter Antarctic winter, when the temperature can drop to -60°C (-76°F).

**Fluffy chicks**
Emperor penguin chicks have downy grey feathers. They stay on the ice, dependent on their parents, until they moult into their adult plumage and set off to sea to fish for themselves.

**Speedy sliders**
Penguins waddle around slowly on land, but they have a way of speeding up – "tobogganing" over snow and ice on their bellies.

SOUTHERN OCEAN

### ANIMALS IN DANGER

**Emperor penguin**
⚠ **IUCN status:** near threatened
⊕ **Population estimate:** 595,000 in 2009

**Keeping warm**
Thousands of males huddle together to stay warm in the harsh Antarctic winter. Each is incubating a single egg under his belly, on top of his feet. The males stay on the ice with their egg all winter, until the females return.

**Galápagos penguin**
All 18 species of penguin live in the southern hemisphere. The most northerly one lives on the Galápagos Islands at the equator, nesting in crevices in the volcanic rock.

**Jackass penguin**
The only African penguin nests and feeds mainly on and around offshore islands, but is also sometimes found on the coasts of Namibia and South Africa.

**Little penguin**
This is the world's smallest penguin, at only 40 cm (16 in) tall. It lives on southern Australian, Tasmanian, and New Zealand coasts, nesting on the dunes.

**Macaroni penguin**
Like most penguin species, the macaroni penguin lives on islands in the Southern Ocean, between Antarctica and warmer waters further north.

**Adélie penguin**
The Adélie penguin is the only other penguin species restricted to Antarctica. Unlike the emperor, it breeds on ice-free shores during the summer months.

# Snowy owl

Few predatory birds are found as far north as the snowy owl. Many other owl species live in cold northern forests, but only the snowy can survive on the treeless tundra, where the ground is frozen solid and covered in snow for much of the year.

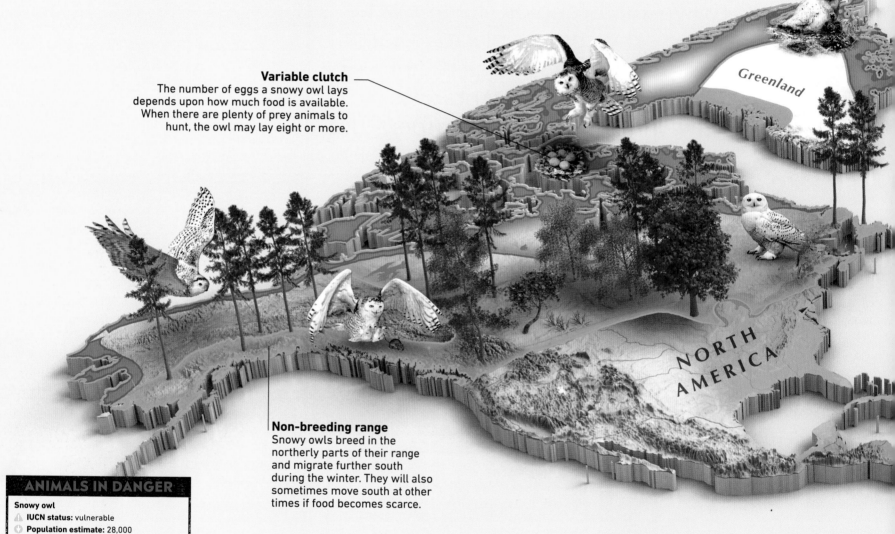

**Ground nester**
Unlike other owls, the snowy owl must nest on the ground in its open tundra habitat. It chooses an elevated site to give it a view of approaching danger.

**Variable clutch**
The number of eggs a snowy owl lays depends upon how much food is available. When there are plenty of prey animals to hunt, the owl may lay eight or more.

Greenland

NORTH AMERICA

**Non-breeding range**
Snowy owls breed in the northerly parts of their range and migrate further south during the winter. They will also sometimes move south at other times if food becomes scarce.

**ANIMALS IN DANGER**

**Snowy owl**
⚠ **IUCN status:** vulnerable
✛ **Population estimate:** 28,000

**Blending in**
The snowy owl is the only owl with an all-white plumage. This helps to disguise it against the snowy ground, especially during the Arctic summer when there is almost continuous daylight and the bird is breeding and hunts at all hours.

**Hunting**
The snowy owl has such good hearing it can detect the position of prey burrowing beneath a blanket of snow. It swallows small rodents whole, but will tear larger animals, such as hares and rabbits, to pieces first.

**Winter habitat**
In winter, migrating snowy owls reach the southernmost parts of their range, where they may hunt ducks and grebes on marshes or moorland, or even rely on carrion.

**Finding food**
Snowy owls regularly move from place to place according to the supply of food. They stay in the same location only if prey is abundant.

ASIA

EUROPE

## Arctic owl

The snowy owl survives and even breeds within the Arctic Circle in Canada, Greenland, and Russia, where it hunts burrowing rodents, such as lemmings and voles. Only during the bitter, dark Arctic winter does it move further south.

AFRICA

Snowy owls have excellent eyesight, like all birds of prey

SOUTH AMERICA

**Barred plumage**
All snowy owls have small, black, bar-like markings. These are more extensive in the larger female – especially on the sides and back.

**Silent wings**
As in other owls, the feathers in the wings of a snowy owl have comb-like fringes, which help to muffle the sound as the wing flaps through the air.

**KEY**
☐ Snowy owl breeding range
▨ Snowy owl non-breeding range

A SNOWY OWL'S **WINGSPAN** MAY BE MORE THAN **1.5m** (5 FT)

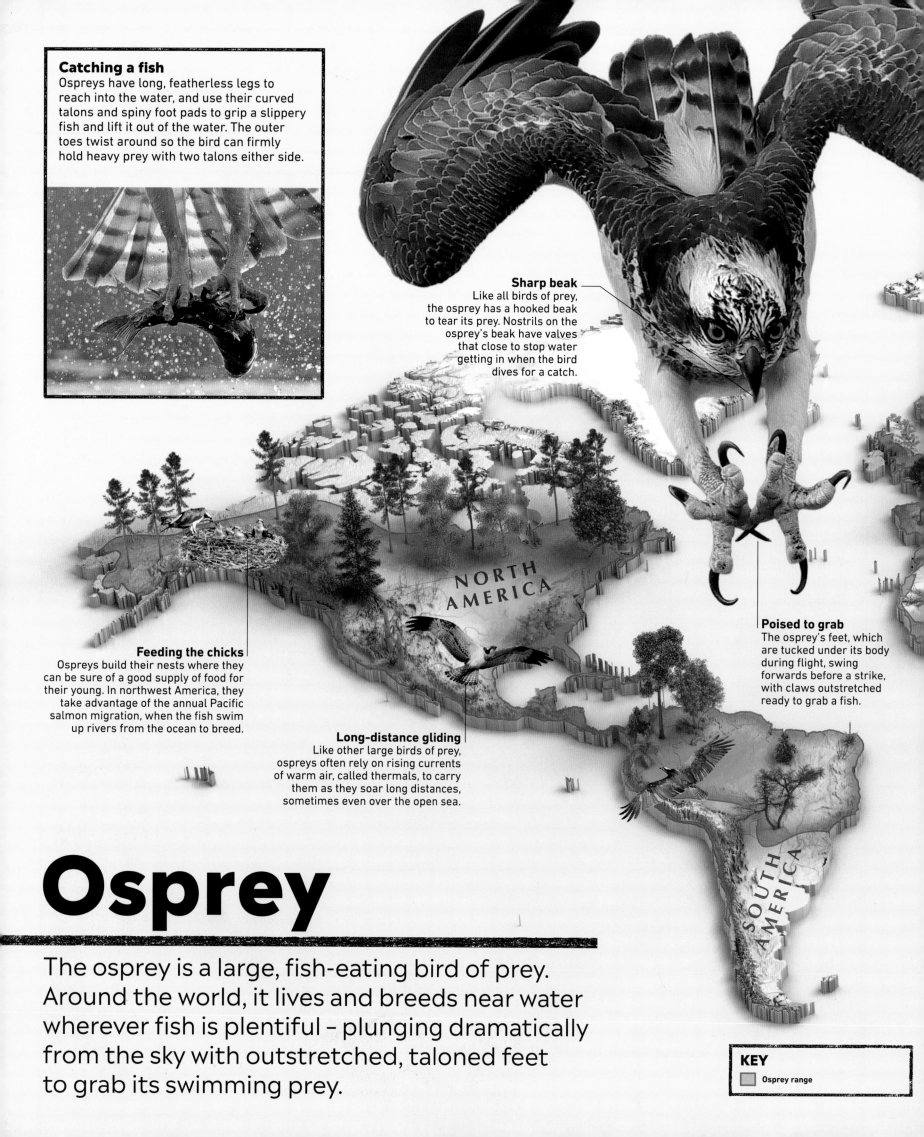

### Catching a fish
Ospreys have long, featherless legs to reach into the water, and use their curved talons and spiny foot pads to grip a slippery fish and lift it out of the water. The outer toes twist around so the bird can firmly hold heavy prey with two talons either side.

### Sharp beak
Like all birds of prey, the osprey has a hooked beak to tear its prey. Nostrils on the osprey's beak have valves that close to stop water getting in when the bird dives for a catch.

### Poised to grab
The osprey's feet, which are tucked under its body during flight, swing forwards before a strike, with claws outstretched ready to grab a fish.

### Feeding the chicks
Ospreys build their nests where they can be sure of a good supply of food for their young. In northwest America, they take advantage of the annual Pacific salmon migration, when the fish swim up rivers from the ocean to breed.

### Long-distance gliding
Like other large birds of prey, ospreys often rely on rising currents of warm air, called thermals, to carry them as they soar long distances, sometimes even over the open sea.

NORTH AMERICA

SOUTH AMERICA

# Osprey

The osprey is a large, fish-eating bird of prey. Around the world, it lives and breeds near water wherever fish is plentiful – plunging dramatically from the sky with outstretched, taloned feet to grab its swimming prey.

KEY

Osprey range

**AN OSPREY CAN CARRY PREY** WEIGHING AROUND **1 KG** (2 LB) – HALF ITS OWN BODY WEIGHT

**AN OSPREY'S WINGSPAN** MAY BE UP TO **1.8 M** (6 FT) WIDE

**Passing through**
In the northern parts of their range, ospreys are seasonal visitors, arriving to hunt and breed in spring and summer, before migrating south to avoid the bitter winters.

**Breeding pair**
Ospreys start breeding at around three years old. Typically, a male mates with a single female, but if he can defend two nests, he might have a second partner.

ASIA

EUROPE

AFRICA

AUSTRALIA

**Year-round residents**
In warmer parts of the world, such as southern Asia, some populations of osprey are resident throughout the year and do not migrate.

**Smaller birds**
The ospreys in Southeast Asia, New Guinea, and Australia are slightly smaller than those in the rest of the world. Some scientists think that they belong to a different species.

**Winter visitors**
Across sub-Saharan Africa, ospreys are winter visitors, travelling from Europe at the end of the northern summer. Only in Egypt and other parts of northeastern Africa are they resident all year.

**Waterside nests**
Ospreys nest along the shores of lakes and rivers or by marshes, typically choosing an exposed tree in which to build a platform of sticks before laying a clutch of three eggs. The first-born chicks are the strongest – younger ones may be left to starve if food is scarce.

**OSPREYS MIGRATING FROM AFRICA TO EUROPE** IN SUMMER TRAVEL UP TO **8,000 KM** (5,000 MILES)

## Worldwide raptor

The osprey is one of the world's most wide-ranging birds. It lives almost everywhere there is water to fish, except for the cold polar regions and the remotest islands. Birds in the northern hemisphere migrate south for the winter, but ospreys around the equator tend to stay in the same place all year round.

**A committee of vultures**
From a rocky peak in the Eastern Rhodopes Mountains, Bulgaria, a group of griffon vultures survey their surroundings for food. These large birds of prey are scavengers – they feed on carrion (dead animals). Using their huge wings, they soar on thermal air currents while scanning the ground for fresh carcasses.

**Colourful plumage**
Like other species of macaw, this parrot has bright colours – blue above and yellow below – but it is surprisingly difficult to spot it when foraging high in the forest canopy.

**Amazonian parrot**
The blue-and-yellow macaw is found throughout the Amazon forest. Here, tall trees provide fruit and nuts for feeding, while the trunks of dead palms offer comfortable holes to nest. This parrot is still common throughout much of the region, but it is becoming threatened by deforestation and the pet trade.

**Long tail**
As well as their large size, reaching up to 86 cm (34 in) in length, macaws are also distinguished from other parrots by their long tapering tail.

**Tools for dining**
Like all parrots, the blue-and-yellow macaw is equipped to pick up and crack open hard-shelled nuts. It uses its clawed feet and a very powerful, but sensitive, beak to grasp and break open nuts. Sometimes, one macaw may try to steal the seed from another.

# Blue-and-yellow macaw

This spectacular bird is one of the biggest of the world's 405 parrot species. The blue-and-yellow macaw flies in noisy flocks over the canopy of the world's largest forest, the Amazon, which covers much of northern South America.

# BLUE-AND-YELLOW MACAWS ARE **NOT ENDANGERED**, BUT THEIR **NUMBERS ARE DECLINING** DUE TO **SHRINKING HABITATS**

# MACAWS ARE HIGHLY PRIZED AS PETS, LEADING **POACHERS** TO TARGET THESE BIRDS AND **SELL THEM ILLEGALLY**

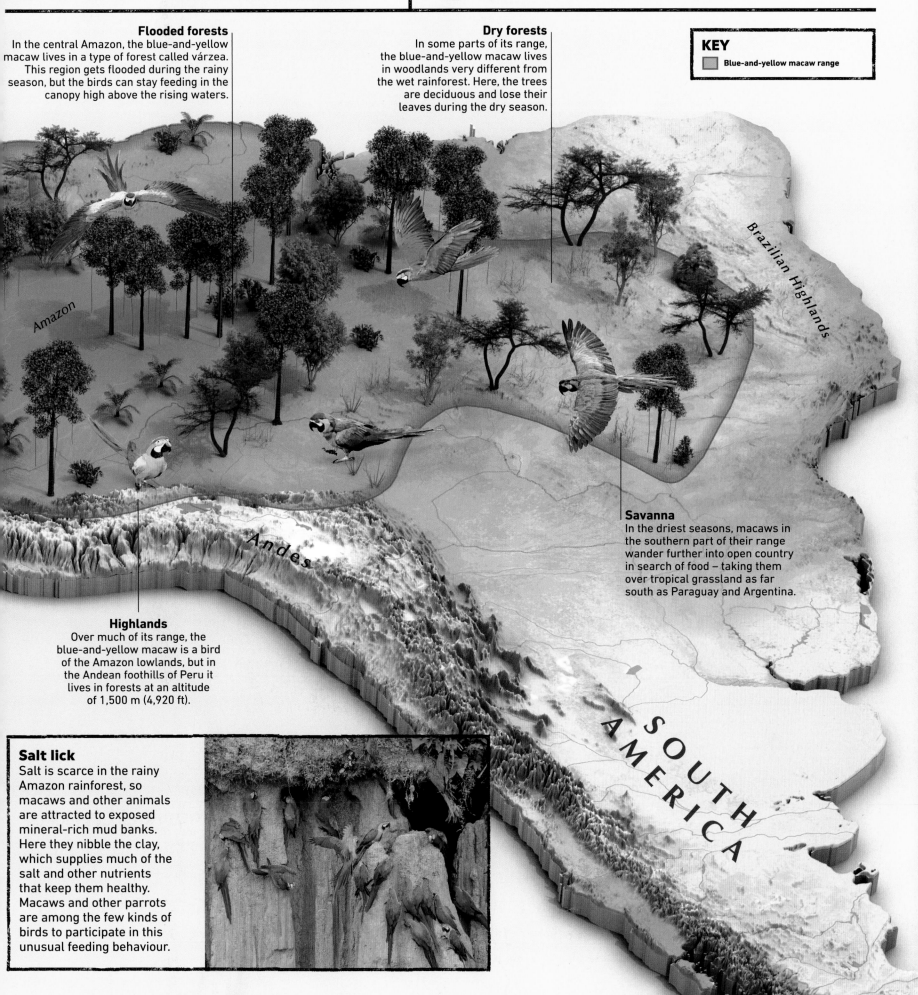

**Flooded forests**
In the central Amazon, the blue-and-yellow macaw lives in a type of forest called várzea. This region gets flooded during the rainy season, but the birds can stay feeding in the canopy high above the rising waters.

**Dry forests**
In some parts of its range, the blue-and-yellow macaw lives in woodlands very different from the wet rainforest. Here, the trees are deciduous and lose their leaves during the dry season.

**KEY**
■ Blue-and-yellow macaw range

**Highlands**
Over much of its range, the blue-and-yellow macaw is a bird of the Amazon lowlands, but in the Andean foothills of Peru it lives in forests at an altitude of 1,500 m (4,920 ft).

**Savanna**
In the driest seasons, macaws in the southern part of their range wander further into open country in search of food – taking them over tropical grassland as far south as Paraguay and Argentina.

**Salt lick**
Salt is scarce in the rainy Amazon rainforest, so macaws and other animals are attracted to exposed mineral-rich mud banks. Here they nibble the clay, which supplies much of the salt and other nutrients that keep them healthy. Macaws and other parrots are among the few kinds of birds to participate in this unusual feeding behaviour.

Amazon

Andes

Brazilian Highlands

SOUTH AMERICA

## Crossing the globe

Barn swallows are found across much of the world and each year most cross the equator in their migrations – between North and South America or the wildest stretches of Asia. Swallows from Europe even travel across Africa's Sahara Desert to reach their wintering grounds.

**NORTH AMERICA**

**North America**
Barn swallows in North America breed from May to August. The swallows here – like those in far eastern Siberia – have reddish-brown, rather than pure white, underparts.

**Caribbean passage**
Swallows migrating south from North America either island-hop through the Caribbean, or follow the path of land through Central America.

**South America**
Barn swallows arriving in South America reach Colombia and the Guianas by late August, and Brazil, Paraguay, and Argentina by September.

**SOUTH AMERICA**

**Europe**
Throughout summer, barn swallows breed across Europe, and as far south as northern Africa. Most of those from northern and central Europe start their migration south in September or October.

**EUROPE**

**AFRICA**

**Africa**
Barn swallows overwinter across vast regions of Africa: birds arriving from western Europe tend to head to the west, and those from eastern Europe to the east. The longest distance travelled between Europe and Africa is an incredible 11,660 km (7,245 miles).

# Barn swallow

More than half of all bird species are small perching birds, or passerines. Many are expert at hunting insects on the wing. Barn swallows nest and raise their young in the northern summers, when the skies are buzzing with life. But they must migrate to the warmer tropics before winter comes and insect numbers fall.

## KEY

- Barn swallow range (breeding and resident)
- Barn swallow range (non-breeding)
- → North American migration
- → European and Western Asian migration
- → Central and East Asian migration

## Wide bill
The bill is short and flat, but can open wide to scoop up insects in flight, or collect mud to make nests.

## Western Asia
To the east, the barn swallow's range extends across Central Asia and Russia. Most of these birds will overwinter in southern Asia.

## Forked tail
For controlled flight, the long tail spreads wide to help the barn swallow slow down.

## Nesting
Many barn swallows attach their mud nests to the walls of buildings such as houses or barns, hence their name. They often line their nests with grasses or feathers, the whole construction taking about ten days to complete.

ASIA

## India
Most barn swallows seen in India are winter visitors only, but further north of this country – and in a few other warmer parts of the world – they may be resident all year.

## Eastern Asia
In this part of the world swallows breed from the Himalayas to Japan. The birds here have creamy-white underparts, but those in far-eastern Siberia have reddish underparts, like those in the Americas.

## Hunting for flies
Barn swallows use their long, pointed wings to manoeuvre themselves in flight. Flying up to 40 km/h (25 mph), these acrobatic birds can turn quickly to snap up insects with a wide, open beak.

## Australia
Barn swallows breeding in eastern Asia typically overwinter in Southeast Asia, but during the twentieth century started migrating further into Australia.

AUSTRALIA

# THESE EXPERT NAVIGATORS
## CAN COVER MORE THAN **320 KM** (200 MILES) **IN A SINGLE DAY**

MAMMALS

# Mammal facts

The first mammals evolved 220 million years ago, when dinosaurs dominated the Earth. Today, mammals have adapted to live almost everywhere and are spread all over the world, from grasslands and rainforests to icy poles and deep oceans.

## WHAT IS A MAMMAL?

**Vertebrates**
Although they may look different, all mammals have an internal skeleton that is made of bone.

**Warm-blooded**
Mammals maintain a stable body temperature, whether they are in a hot or cold environment.

**Live young**
Most mammals give birth to live young, rather than hatching from eggs like birds.

**Drink milk**
Young mammals feed on milk from their mother, which provides vital nutrients for their growth.

**Hair**
Mammals have fur, spines, or scales to trap heat. Marine mammals have insulating blubber.

## MAMMAL TYPES

**ESTIMATED NUMBER OF MAMMAL SPECIES: 6,550**

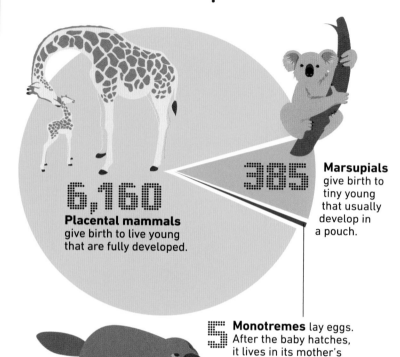

**6,160**
**Placental mammals**
give birth to live young that are fully developed.

**385**
**Marsupials**
give birth to tiny young that usually develop in a pouch.

**5**
**Monotremes** lay eggs. After the baby hatches, it lives in its mother's pouch for several weeks as it continues to develop.

## THE TAILLESS TENREC OF MADAGASCAR CAN HAVE UP TO 32 BABIES IN ONE LITTER.

## EXTREME HABITATS

Some hardy mammals have adapted to survive in extremely hot, cold, or rather odd places.

**Musk oxen** use their hooves to dig through snow and find edible plants in temperatures below freezing. They live mainly in the tundra regions of Greenland and Arctic North America.

**Kangaroo rats** have adapted to live in the extreme heat of the deserts in western USA and Mexico. This rodent does not drink water, instead getting moisture from desert grass seeds.

**Goats** can grip tiny crevices with their hooves, allowing them to ascend a vertical cliff safely. These rock-climbing goats are in Greece, but this mammal can be found all over the world.

## INDONESIA IS HOME TO

**291 MAMMAL SPECIES**

MORE THAN ANY OTHER **COUNTRY.**

# BIGGEST MAMMAL

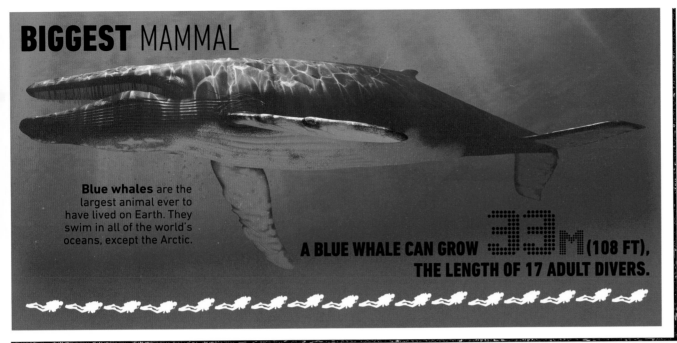

**Blue whales** are the largest animal ever to have lived on Earth. They swim in all of the world's oceans, except the Arctic.

A BLUE WHALE CAN GROW **33m** (108 FT), THE LENGTH OF 17 ADULT DIVERS.

# SMALLEST MAMMAL

The **Kitti's hog-nosed bat** lives in limestone caves near rivers in parts of Thailand and Myanmar.

ITS HEAD–BODY LENGTH IS UP TO **34** MM (1⅜ IN) – TWICE AS LONG AS A BUMBLEBEE.

# FASTEST MAMMALS

Whether on water, land, or in the air, these mammals are some of the fastest in the animal kingdom.

**IN WATER:** ORCA AT **88 KM/H** (55 MPH)

**ON LAND:** CHEETAH AT **113 KM/H** (70 MPH)

**IN THE AIR:** BRAZILIAN FREE-TAILED BAT AT **160 KM/H** (100 MPH)

This speedy bat is found in parts of North, Central, and South America.

# LONGEST OVERLAND MIGRATION

CARIBOU MIGRATION IS A RETURN TRIP OF MORE THAN **1,200** KM (745 MILES)

**Caribou** are native to North America, and spend summer months in the north of the continent feeding on grasses. This is also where females give birth. When winter snow falls, they head south in search of grazing.

# DEEPEST DIVE

**Cuvier's beaked whales** are found worldwide. The record-breaking dive of this mammal reached a depth equal to the height of **3.5 Burj Khalifa** buildings.

The **Burj Khalfia** in Dubai, UAE, is the world's tallest building, at a height of **830 m** (2,720 ft).

**CUVIER'S BEAKED WHALE 2,992** m (9,816 FT)

# SMART MAMMALS

**Bottlenose dolphins** in Shark Bay, Australia, use protective marine sponges (an invertebrate) to disturb sandy seafloors filled with potential prey, such as spothead grubfish. It is thought that only females do this, and they pass on this useful fishing skill to their daughters.

# LONG JUMPER

**WHITE-HANDED GIBBONS** OF **SOUTHEAST ASIA** CAN JUMP **12** m (40 FT) FROM BRANCH TO BRANCH.

# Egg-laying mammals

Some mammals lay eggs instead of giving birth to live young. These are the monotremes, found only in Australia and the island of New Guinea. They include the duck-billed platypus and four species of spiny-coated echidnas.

**Sir David's long-beaked echidna**
This species lives in a tiny area of a mountain range in Indonesia. Only one specimen has ever been found in the wild.

INDONESIA

**Western long-beaked echidna**
Long-beaked echidnas from hotter lowlands look spinier because they have less insulating fur than those that live in cooler highlands.

## Highly adaptable

Monotremes inhabit a wide variety of habitats, from Australia's arid deserts to the snow-covered mountains of Papua New Guinea. Short-beaked echidnas are the most adaptable and have the largest range, while the other monotremes are limited to smaller areas.

Arnhem Land

Tanami Desert

**Eastern long-beaked echidna**

**Spiny coat**
An echidna's coat is made up of protective spines interspersed with fur. If threatened, the echidna can roll into a spiky ball.

**Short-beaked echidna**
This adaptable monotreme is the only species that lives in the dry, arid interior of Australia, known as the "outback".

Gibson Desert

Great Victoria Desert

**Toothless feeding**
All monotremes lack teeth, and instead have sensitive beaks for catching invertebrate prey. Echidnas dig through soil with sharp claws to expose prey and use their long, sticky tongue to trap them. The platypus uses its sensitive bill to find shellfish buried in the mud, then crushes them with horny plates inside its bill.

**Forest dwellers**
In the forests of western Australia, short-beaked echidnas make their homes among rocks, in the spaces between tree roots, and inside hollow logs.

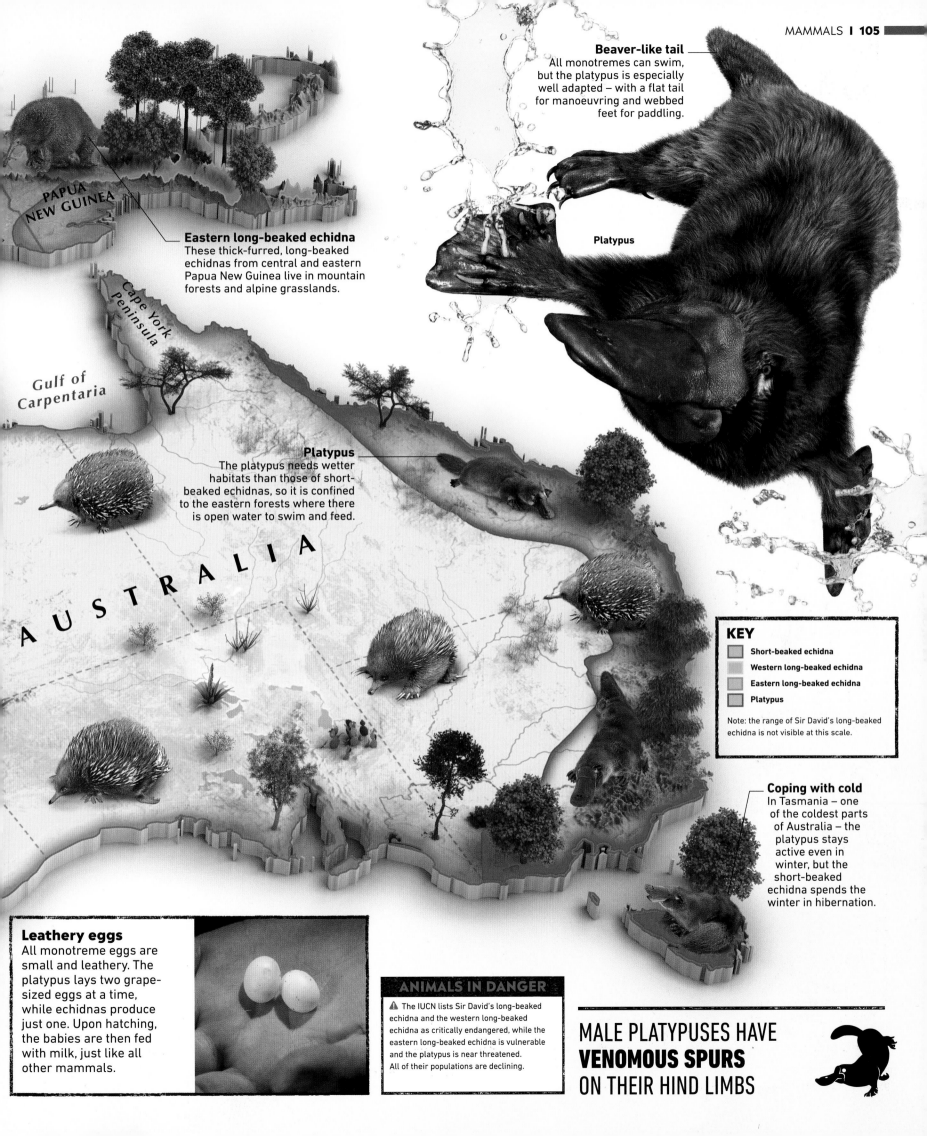

**Beaver-like tail**
All monotremes can swim, but the platypus is especially well adapted – with a flat tail for manoeuvring and webbed feet for paddling.

Platypus

**Eastern long-beaked echidna**
These thick-furred, long-beaked echidnas from central and eastern Papua New Guinea live in mountain forests and alpine grasslands.

PAPUA NEW GUINEA

Cape York Peninsula

Gulf of Carpentaria

**Platypus**
The platypus needs wetter habitats than those of short-beaked echidnas, so it is confined to the eastern forests where there is open water to swim and feed.

A U S T R A L I A

**KEY**

| | |
|---|---|
| ▨ | Short-beaked echidna |
| ▨ | Western long-beaked echidna |
| ▨ | Eastern long-beaked echidna |
| ▨ | Platypus |

Note: the range of Sir David's long-beaked echidna is not visible at this scale.

**Coping with cold**
In Tasmania – one of the coldest parts of Australia – the platypus stays active even in winter, but the short-beaked echidna spends the winter in hibernation.

**Leathery eggs**
All monotreme eggs are small and leathery. The platypus lays two grape-sized eggs at a time, while echidnas produce just one. Upon hatching, the babies are then fed with milk, just like all other mammals.

**ANIMALS IN DANGER**

⚠ The IUCN lists Sir David's long-beaked echidna and the western long-beaked echidna as critically endangered, while the eastern long-beaked echidna is vulnerable and the platypus is near threatened. All of their populations are declining.

**MALE PLATYPUSES HAVE VENOMOUS SPURS ON THEIR HIND LIMBS**

# KOALAS SLEEP UP TO 20 HOURS EACH DAY

18-20 HRS

**KEY**

▢ Koala range

Cape York Peninsula

Gulf of Carpentaria

A U S T R A L I A

### Keeping cool
In northeastern Australia, where the climate is very hot, koalas have shorter, paler, fur to help keep them cool.

### Facing forwards
The koala is the only marsupial with forward-facing eyes. This makes it a better judge of distance, which is important for clambering through branches without falling.

### Following eucalyptus
Though koalas are found in a range of habitats, from subtropical forests to grasslands and savannas, their range is dependent on the presence of eucalyptus trees, the leaves of which make up the large majority of their diet. Much of their habitat has been lost due to logging, forest clearing, and bushfires, putting many koala populations at risk of extinction.

### Tough digestion
The leaves of eucalyptus are hard and fibrous, making them very difficult to digest. They quickly fill the stomach of a browsing koala, but provide little nutrition, meaning that when they are not eating or sleeping, koalas spend their time resting to conserve energy.

# Koala

Found only in the eucalyptus forests of Australia, koalas belong to a group of mammals called marsupials. Unlike most other mammals, marsupials give birth to tiny young that do most of their growing outside their mother's body – usually in a pouch.

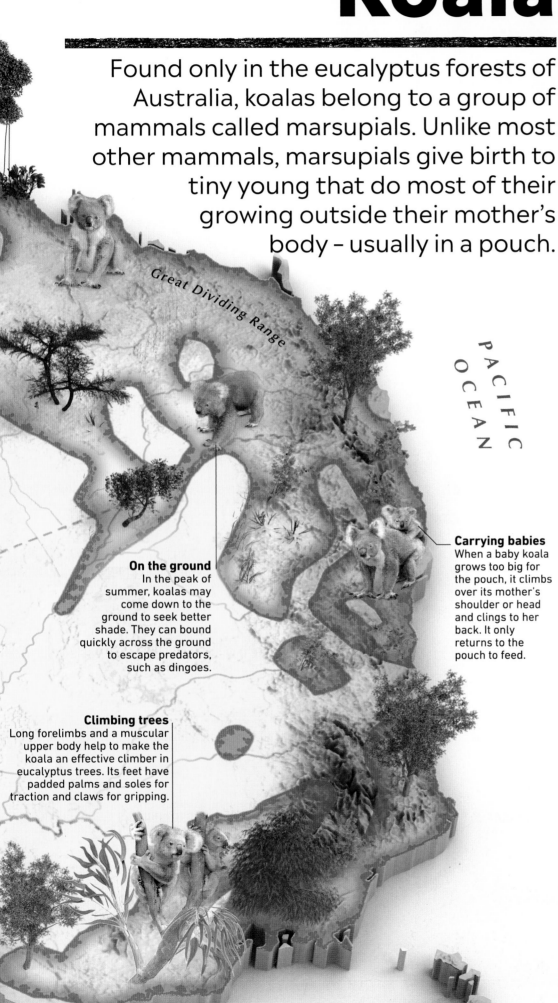

Great Dividing Range

PACIFIC OCEAN

**On the ground**
In the peak of summer, koalas may come down to the ground to seek better shade. They can bound quickly across the ground to escape predators, such as dingoes.

**Carrying babies**
When a baby koala grows too big for the pouch, it climbs over its mother's shoulder or head and clings to her back. It only returns to the pouch to feed.

**Climbing trees**
Long forelimbs and a muscular upper body help to make the koala an effective climber in eucalyptus trees. Its feet have padded palms and soles for traction and claws for gripping.

**Red kangaroo**
The largest species of kangaroo is well adapted to cope with Australia's dry interior, and ranges widely over the semi-deserts of the country.

**Goodfellow's tree kangaroo**
In the tropical rainforests of New Guinea, Goodfellow's tree kangaroos have evolved to climb through the branches.

**Virginia opossum**
There are 120 species of opossums, mostly found in tropical South and Central America. Only the Virginia opossum ranges into temperate North America.

**Tasmanian devil**
The carnivorous Tasmanian devil used to be widespread across all of Australia, but is now restricted to the southern island of Tasmania.

**Bear cuscus**
Living in tropical lowland forests on the Indonesian island of Sulawesi, the bear cuscus is the most western-dwelling marsupial in Australasia and Oceania.

**Nine-banded armadillo**
This armadillo is common in the woodlands of the southern United States, but is also found in much of South America. It forages for fruit, worms, and eggs as well as insects.

**American range**
Armadillos range from the southern parts of North America, which is home only to the nine-banded armadillo, to as far south as the grasslands of Argentina. Most species prefer moist habitats, where they can find plenty of termites, ants, and beetles to eat.

NORTH AMERICA

**Widespread range**
In Central America, the nine-banded armadillo lives high up in mountain forests.

# Armadillos

Closely related to sloths and anteaters, these armoured mammals are found only in the Americas and nowhere else. Of the 21 existing armadillo species, five are shown here. They are the only mammals with bony armour, and they use their heightened sense of smell and long, sticky tongue to catch insects and other small animals.

**Bony armour**
The armour of an armadillo is made up of bony plates covered with tough, horny skin. The plates are connected loosely to give the body the flexibility to move.

Southern three-banded armadillo

**WHEN STARTLED**, THE NINE-BANDED ARMADILLO MAY **JUMP MORE THAN 1 M (3 FT)** INTO THE AIR

## KEY

- Nine-banded armadillo
- Giant armadillo
- Hairy long-nosed armadillo
- Southern three-banded armadillo
- Pink fairy armadillo

## Burrowing down

All armadillos are burrowers, and use their strong clawed feet to dig tunnels with sleeping chambers. Most species spend much of the day in their burrows to avoid the heat of the sun or to hide from large predators, such as pumas.

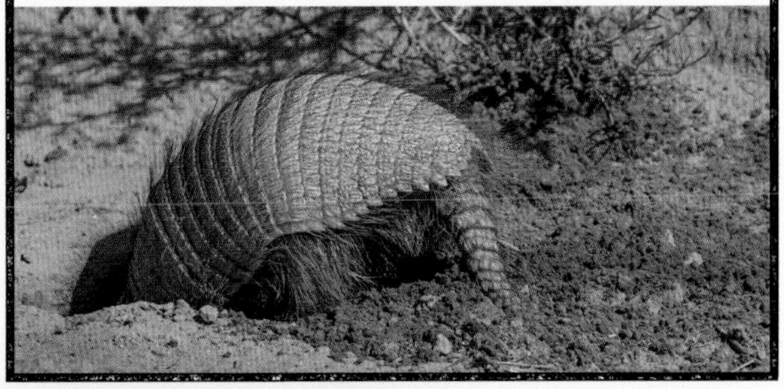

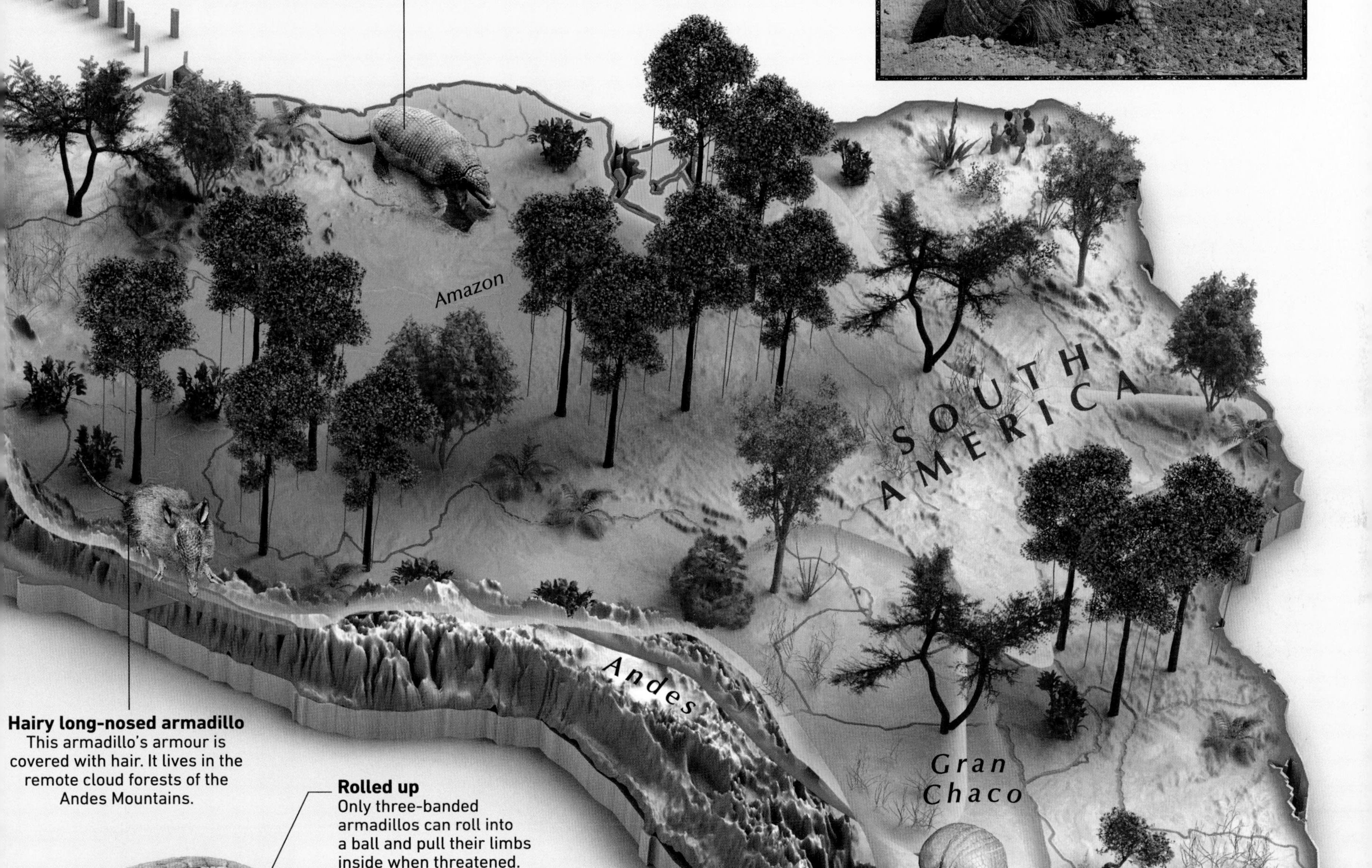

### Giant armadillo

The Amazon Basin is home to the biggest species of armadillo. The 130-lb (60-kg) giant armadillo lives in undisturbed tropical forests. It is hunted for its meat and threatened by deforestation.

ATLANTIC OCEAN

Amazon

SOUTH AMERICA

### Hairy long-nosed armadillo

This armadillo's armour is covered with hair. It lives in the remote cloud forests of the Andes Mountains.

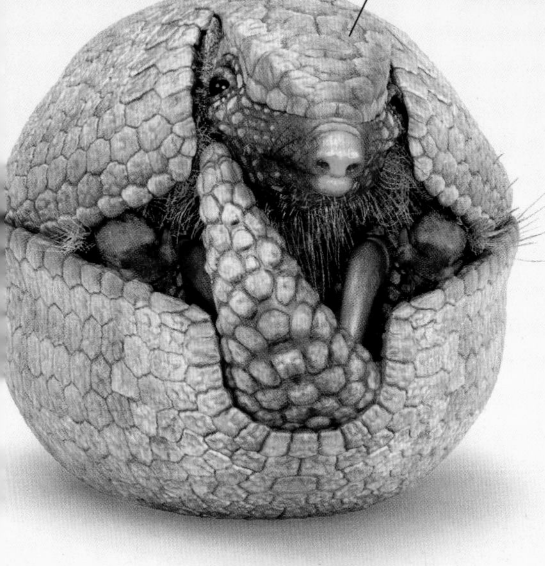

### Rolled up

Only three-banded armadillos can roll into a ball and pull their limbs inside when threatened.

Andes

Gran Chaco

### Southern three-banded armadillo

This species is found in drier habitats than most other armadillos. It lives in the thorny forest, scrub, and savanna of the Gran Chaco – a wide grassy area in central South America.

### Pink fairy armadillo

The mole-like pink fairy armadillo is the smallest armadillo species. Its body ends with a vertical rump plate, which it uses to compact sand in burrows or even seal their entrance when danger threatens.

# Brown-throated sloth

Few animals are so tied to life in trees as the sloth. These plant-eaters climb the branches with slow, deliberate movements and have long arms and claws that act as grappling hooks. There are six species of sloths living in tropical American forests, but the brown-throated sloth is the most common.

Guiana Highlands

Amazon

Amazon Basin

Andes

**Afternoon activity**
Sloths are most active in the mid-afternoon, when the warmth of the sun helps to power their slow bodies, and they often move to sunnier branches to sunbathe.

**Living upside down**
In most mammals, hanging upside down puts pressure on the lungs. But sloths have adapted to this position, allowing them to move more easily through their habitat. They have fibres that attach their inner organs to their lower ribs, holding the organs in place so they don't crush the lungs.

**Ground crawler**
On the rare occasions when the brown-throated sloth leaves the safe haven of the trees, it is able to crawl across the ground by pulling forwards with one forearm and the opposite hindfoot at the same time.

**KEY**
Brown-throated sloth range

**Trips to the loo**
The brown-throated sloth descends from the trees for just one reason: to poo. Once a week, it makes its way down to the forest floor, digs a small depression with its short tail, and defecates. It then covers the dung with leaf litter and climbs back up. If forced to do so, a sloth can crawl along the ground using the soles of its front and back feet, but will soon make for the nearest tree to return to the safety of the canopy.

**Living together**
Algae that grow on the fur of the brown-throated sloth tinge its fur green, helping to disguise it among the leaves. The algae are fertilized by the droppings of a species of moth that lives only in the sloth's fur. When the sloth descends to the ground to poo, the moths briefly leave the sloth's fur to lay their eggs, and their larvae feed on the dung.

**Climbing trees**
Sloths climb up and down trees by hugging the tree trunk. When moving horizontally, they hang upside down from the branches.

**Leafy diet**
Sloths move slowly because the rainforest leaves of their diet don't contain many nutrients. The little energy they gain from their diet is needed for both getting around and digestion.

Brazilian Highlands

Paraguay

Paraná

**Water absorbent**
The dense fur of a sloth absorbs a lot of water when it rains. It is thought that a water-soaked coat helps to protect it from extreme temperatures.

Atacama Desert

SOUTH AMERICA

## Life in trees

These slow-moving tree dwellers live in the dense tropical rainforest canopies of Central and South America. They are able to eat the leaves of around 50 species of rainforest tree, but individuals tend to spend most of their time in a single tree that contains their favourite leaves.

**Western ranges**
African savanna elephants in western grasslands are widely scattered and isolated from other savanna elephants.

AFRICA

**Sharing habitats**
In open woodland and forest edges of parts of Central Africa, it is likely that African forest and African savanna elephants live together in similar habitats.

*Red Sea*

*Gulf of Guinea*

**African forest elephant**
These elephants are smaller than African savanna elephants. The largest groups occur where the forest is broken up with patches of savanna.

*Horn of Africa*

African savanna elephant

**African savanna elephant**
Most African savanna elephants live in dry woodland and shrubland, but in more arid parts of the continent they reach into deserts – as long as they have access to pools of water.

**Large ears**
Both species of African elephants have much bigger ears than those of Asian elephants. Blood circulating through them is cooled as the ears are waved back and forth.

# Elephants

These giants are the world's heaviest land animal. They are well known for their long trunks and mighty tusks. Two of the three existing species can be found in fragmented ranges around Africa, while their smaller cousins inhabit the tropical forests of Southeast Asia.

# 20,000 AFRICAN ELEPHANTS ARE KILLED EACH YEAR FOR THE ILLEGAL IVORY TRADE

# THE AFRICAN ELEPHANT POPULATION HAS DROPPED BY 90% OVER THE LAST 100 YEARS

## ANIMALS IN DANGER

**African forest elephant**
⚠ IUCN status: endangered
⊕ Population estimate: 100,000

**African savanna elephant**
⚠ IUCN status: vulnerable
⊕ Population estimate: 315,000

**Asian elephant**
⚠ IUCN status: endangered
⊕ Population estimate: 20,000–40,000

ASIA

*Arabian Sea*

INDIA

CHINA

*Bay of Bengal*

*South China Sea*

INDONESIA

## Habitats at risk

From the savannas, open woodlands, and shrublands of Africa to the grasslands and humid forests of Asia, elephants are a key part of their ecosystems. But human intervention is leading to the destruction of their natural habitats, putting them at risk of extinction.

### Asian elephant

In mainland Asia – including India – elephants live in grassland or forest. Their natural ranges are shrinking, leaving them access to only 15 per cent of their original range.

### Domed head

Asian elephants are smaller than their African cousins and have a two-domed, rather than single-domed, forehead. Their skin is also smoother and hairier than the rough skin of African elephants.

### Smaller sizes

Asian elephants living in forests in Borneo are shorter than those on the mainland. They are sometimes called Bornean pygmy elephants.

## KEY

▢ African forest elephant
▢ African savanna elephant
▢ Asian elephant

**Asian elephant**

## Spreading seeds

Elephant herds can flatten foliage and tear down trees, but they also help scatter seeds. They eat ripe fruit from their favourite trees, and the seeds pass out in piles of fertilizing dung.

## Tree browsers

Elephants are not picky eaters – they browse on leaves, seeds, fruit, flowers, grass, and tree bark. They will even push over trees to get at the nutritious roots deep underground.

# Eurasian red squirrel

Around 90 species of tree squirrel live in forests around the world. Among them is the Eurasian red squirrel, which dwells in cool northern forests. Unlike most rodents, bushy-tailed squirrels are active during the day and they can often be spotted climbing trees.

**Competing squirrels**
In Britain, the introduced eastern grey squirrel has displaced the red squirrel from most of its original range (see panel below). It now survives only in places where grey squirrel numbers are controlled.

EUROPE

**Raising babies**
In spring, female squirrels give birth to litters of up to six kits in tree holes or dreys (nests) made from twigs and leaves in the forest canopy.

**Expansive forests**
Red squirrels survive best in big expanses of forest. In places where forests are fragmented, their numbers drop.

**Outcompeted**
In parts of Europe, such as the UK and Italy, the eastern grey squirrel, introduced from North America, has driven out the native red squirrel because it is stronger and spreads a virus that can be lethal to its red cousins.

**Squirrelling nuts away**
In autumn, the red squirrel stores pinecones, acorns, nuts, and seeds by burying them. It uses memory and a good sense of smell to find them, even under snow in winter, helping it to stay active and keep feeding.

**Bushy-tailed rodent**
The Eurasian red squirrel has a wide range, from western Europe to Siberia. It feeds on tree seeds, especially pine nuts. Its long, bushy tail can be used as a windbreak when the squirrel is feeding, or as shelter from rain or hot sun.

A **RED SQUIRREL** CAN **JUMP UP TO 2 M** (6½ FT) BETWEEN TREES – **10 TIMES ITS OWN BODY LENGTH**

**IN BRITAIN,** THERE ARE AN ESTIMATED **140,000 RED SQUIRRELS,** COMPARED TO **2.5 MILLION GREY SQUIRRELS**

**Social dynamics**
Red squirrels spend most of their time alone, but will huddle in groups in nests on cold nights, or gather together when food is plentiful.

**Cold taiga habitat**
Across Siberia, the red squirrel lives in the great taiga forest: a vast expanse of pine and spruce trees on the edge of the cold Arctic region.

**Coniferous habitats**
Pine seeds are a favourite of red squirrels, so they are especially abundant in pine forests. They hoard pinecones, seeds, and nuts as a winter store – particularly when food crops are low during the coldest months.

**Tufted ears**
Red squirrels have distinctive tufts of fur on their ears, which grow longer in winter months.

**Staying active**
Even in the coldest winters, red squirrels do not hibernate for long periods, as many small mammals do. Instead, they may stay snug in their nests in bitter weather.

ASIA

**Chisel-like teeth**
Like other rodents, red squirrels have chisel-like front incisor teeth. They use these to bite into the woody shells of nuts to reach the nutritious seed inside.

**Colourful fur**
Most red squirrels have reddish-brown fur with a white underside, but some individuals are black, brown, grey, or even blueish.

**KEY**
Eurasian red squirrel range

**Desert rodent**
The elusive long-eared jerboa inhabits the deserts and shrublands that stretch between southern Mongolia and northern China. Its elongated feet help it to hop around the desert sand and leap into the air to catch insects. The large surface area of the jerboa's ears helps to keep it cool by radiating heat from its body.

# Star-nosed mole

With its hyper-sensitive nose and lightning fast reflexes, this unique North American mole is a highly successful hunter of small invertebrates such as worms, insects, and spiders. It spends most of its life in its intricate system of burrows, where it rests, builds nests for rearing young, stores food, and traps prey.

**NORTH AMERICA**

## Western barrier
The star-nosed mole relies on wet habitats to feed and survive, so the western border of its range ends where the drier central prairies of North America begin.

*Lake Superi*

## Wet habitats
The star-nosed mole lives in a range of habitats across eastern North America, including coniferous and deciduous forests, swamps, peat bogs, and along the banks of streams, lakes, and ponds. It prefers to build its burrows in water-logged ground, and relies on its sense of smell to detect prey underground.

## KEY
■ Star-nosed mole range

## Mole hill
Most of its life is spent in underground burrows, but occasionally the star-nosed mole heads to the surface through mole hills in order to hunt prey at night.

## Semi-aquatic mammals
Star-nosed moles are excellent swimmers, and many of their burrows open underwater. They use their highly sensitive nose to hunt for prey – such as aquatic insect larvae, snails, and shrimp – in the waterbed. The rest of their burrow system is built above the water level to prevent flooding.

Mole hill

Some burrows have underwater exits

Nest chamber for rearing young

THERE ARE **25,000 TOUCH SENSORS** ON THE **TENTACLES** OF A STAR-NOSED MOLE

STAR-NOSED MOLES EAT **50% OF THEIR BODY WEIGHT** IN PREY ANIMALS **EACH DAY**

**Sociable moles**
Star-nosed moles are probably more sociable than other species of moles, and occasionally form loose colonies. They mate in the autumn and live together until the babies are born in the spring.

**Northern mole**
At the northernmost reaches of its range, the star-nosed mole lives in the coniferous forests of Canada's cold taiga.

Lake Huron

Lake Erie

Appalachian Mountains

**Up high**
In the Appalachian Mountains, the star-nosed mole is found at altitudes of more than 1,600 m (5,250 ft).

**Nose tentacles**
The nostrils of most star-nosed moles are surrounded by 22 little tentacles – each measuring up to 4 mm (5/32 in) long.

**Catching prey**
With the help of its super sensitive nose, the star-nosed mole is perfectly adapted for finding tiny prey in the water-soaked ground. The fleshy tentacles around the mole's nose are packed with thousands of touch sensors, and it can take less than a fifth of a second for the mole to detect and grab each morsel.

# Lemurs

There are more than 100 species of lemur, and all of them are found only on the island of Madagascar and nowhere else. The five ranges on this map represent a small sample of these isolated primates, and they all heavily depend on their forest habitats for survival.

## 50 SILKY SIFAKAS ARE LEFT IN THE **WILD** – THEY ARE ONE OF THE **RAREST PRIMATES IN THE WORLD**

### Spiny tree habitat
Thorny forests in the dry south of Madagascar – where spiny trees grow like giant cactuses – are home to particular kinds of lemurs, such as Verreaux's sifaka. They have padded palms and soles on their hands and feet, allowing them to leap from trunk to trunk without injury.

### Red-tailed sportive lemur
Despite its name, this species is not very active. Restricted to a tiny area of dry deciduous forest between two rivers, individuals rarely travel more than 1 km (⅗ mile) from their home range. When their habitats are deforested, they are unlikely to move to distant trees.

### Verreaux's sifaka
The powerful thighs of a sifaka – good for leaping from tree to tree – are also used for bounding across the ground or along horizontal branches. They live in forest habitats, including tropical rainforest and spiny dry forest.

### Fat-tailed dwarf lemur
This dwarf lemur endures Madagascar's dry winter season by entering a hibernation-like state and surviving on the stores of fat in its tail. Though its range is small, it is one of the few lemur species with an abundant population.

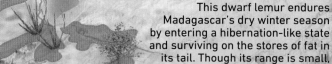

### Ring-tailed lemur
The ring-tailed lemur is found only in Madagascar's dry southern forests and arid open areas. It spends 70 per cent of its time on the ground, more than any other lemur species.

## ANIMALS IN DANGER
⚠ IUCN lists 34 lemur species as critically endangered, including the red-tailed sportive lemur and Verreaux's sifaka, and 45 as endangered, including the ring-tailed lemur and aye-aye. Most others are vulnerable.

## KEY

- Verreaux's sifaka
- Red-tailed sportive lemur
- Fat-tailed dwarf lemur
- Ring-tailed lemur
- Aye-aye

INDIAN OCEAN

MADAGASCAR

## Lemurs in danger

Each species of lemur is adapted to live in a different type of forest habitat, from the ring-tailed lemur in the dry forests of the south to the rainforest-dependent aye-aye. Because many lemurs are restricted to tiny areas of habitat, they are increasingly vulnerable to threats such as deforestation.

**WEIGHING ONLY 31 g (1 OZ), MADAME BERTHE'S MOUSE LEMUR IS THE SMALLEST PRIMATE IN THE WORLD**

### Tail flag
The long, striped tail of a ring-tailed lemur is a visual signal. When travelling in their group, lemurs wave their tails like a flag to help keep members together.

### Aye-aye
This nocturnal lemur can be found in the rainforests of eastern Madagascar. Despite being rare wherever it occurs, the aye-aye could be one of the widest-ranging lemur species.

### Wet nose
Lemurs have forward-facing eyes like related monkeys, but differ from monkeys in having a more pointed, wet nose – good for sniffing scents, especially at night.

### Hunting for woodworm
The aye-aye is a highly specialized feeder. It preys on invertebrates, such as fleshy wood-boring grubs, which live inside tree branches. By tapping a branch and listening to the echo, it can detect if a grub is inside. It gnaws a hole in the wood and hooks the grub out with a specially adapted spindly finger.

Ring-tailed lemur

# Japanese macaque

Most of the more than 330 species of monkeys around the world live in the hot tropics, but the Japanese macaque tolerates the cold. In Japanese forests, it lives further north than any other non-human primate, sometimes ranging high up into cold mountains with heavy winter snowfall.

**Southern monkeys**
In the thick warm forests of southern Japan, macaques spend about half their time on the ground and half in the branches, where they feed on fruit and leaves as well as small animals and eggs.

**Group living**
Across their range, Japanese macaques live in large social groups that can include more than 100 individuals. Groups are bigger where the monkeys are deliberately fed by visiting humans.

**Motherly care**
Female macaques give birth to a single baby after a pregnancy of about 5½ months. The youngster stays in the care of its mother for up to a year.

*Chugoku Mountains*

*Kyushu*

*Shikoku*

**In the highlands**
Although they were once more widespread, today Japanese macaques are mostly found in highland areas, having been hunted elsewhere because of their raids on crops.

**Island monkey**
The Japanese macaque lives on the main Japanese islands of Honshu, Shikoku, and Kyushu. In the southern parts of its range this monkey lives in warm, temperate evergreen forest, but it also inhabits temperate deciduous forest further north.

**Beach monkeys**
On the tiny Japanese island of Koshima, off the coast of Kyushu, Japanese macaques have learned skills that get passed down as youngsters copy adults. On beaches, the monkeys wash food such as sweet potatoes in the sea, and separate lighter grains of wheat from heavier sand by letting the grains float upwards in the water.

THE JAPANESE MACAQUE **CAN SURVIVE** IN TEMPERATURES AS LOW AS **-15°C** (5°F)

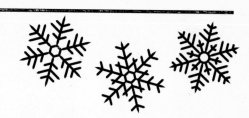

**Northernmost range**
No wild monkey in the world lives further north than the Japanese macaque. Like macaques in the central mountains, they keep warm by bathing in hot springs.

Hokkaido

Ou Mountains

**Snow monkey**
Japanese macaques living in the snowy mountains of central Honshu – close to ski resorts – have become a popular tourist attraction.

Hida Mountains

JAPAN

Honshu

PACIFIC OCEAN

**Hot springs**
In the mountains of central Honshu, temperatures plunge below freezing in the winter. Here, Japanese macaques survive the cold by regularly bathing in thermal pools that are common in this volcanic region.

**Naked face**
Pink skin shows through a very fine coating of fur on the face of an adult macaque, encircled by long, pale whiskers.

**Deciduous forests**
In the northern parts of their range, Japanese macaques range into mountainous areas with deciduous trees – trees that lose their leaves during the winter. At this time of year, macaques move to lower elevations, where there is more food.

**Thick fur**
The greyish fur grows especially long and thick on its back and sides, which helps to trap body heat. The monkey moults its coat in late spring so its fur is shorter in the summertime.

**KEY**

Japanese macaque range

## ANIMALS IN DANGER

**Chimpanzee**
⚠ **IUCN status:** endangered
⊕ **Population estimate:** 340,000–430,000

**Bonobo**
⚠ **IUCN status:** endangered
⊕ **Population estimate:** unknown

**Western gorilla**
⚠ **IUCN status:** critically endangered
⊕ **Population estimate:** 316,000

**Eastern gorilla**
⚠ **IUCN status:** critically endangered
⊕ **Population estimate:** fewer than 5,000

## KEY

- Chimpanzee
- Bonobo
- Western gorilla
- Eastern gorilla

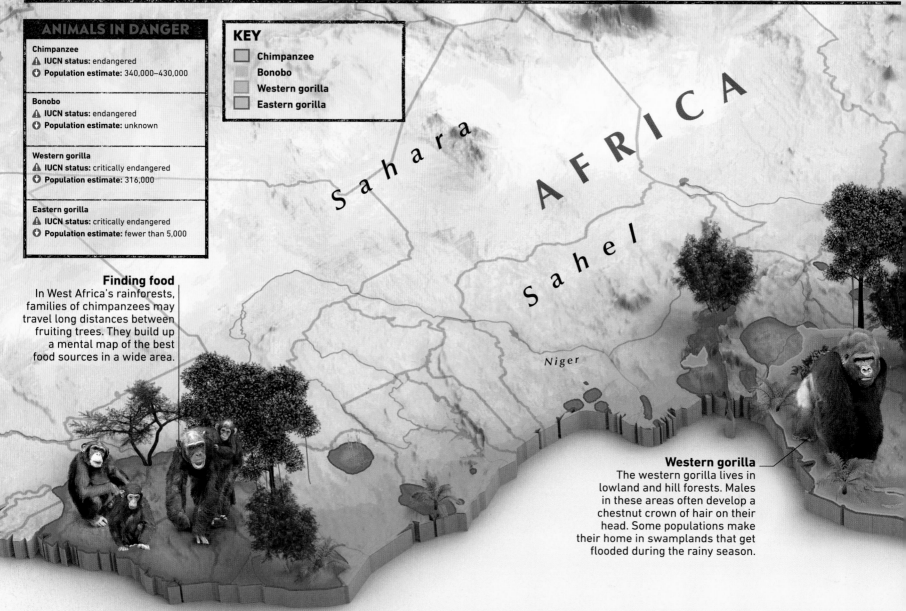

**Finding food**
In West Africa's rainforests, families of chimpanzees may travel long distances between fruiting trees. They build up a mental map of the best food sources in a wide area.

**Western gorilla**
The western gorilla lives in lowland and hill forests. Males in these areas often develop a chestnut crown of hair on their head. Some populations make their home in swamplands that get flooded during the rainy season.

*Map labels: Sahara, AFRICA, Sahel, Niger*

**Green living**
Great apes use branches and foliage to build nests for sleeping at night, and sometimes for resting during the day. Chimpanzee and bonobo nests are built high in trees but gorillas, who are heavier, often nest on the ground, like the one seen here.

# Great apes

The great apes are our closest animal relatives. All great ape species, except the orangutans (see pp.126–127), are found on the continent of Africa. Living in sociable groups in forests around the equator, chimpanzees and bonobos spend more time in trees, while gorillas stay mainly on the ground.

## Chimpanzee
Like other great apes, the chimpanzee walks on its knuckles when on all fours. In the eastern part of its range, it roams central highland forests as high up as 2,790 m (9,155 ft).

## Eastern gorilla
Eastern gorillas have thicker, blacker fur than western gorillas. Some live in lowland habitats, but eastern mountain gorillas live at heights of up to 3,800 m (12,470 ft); they are the stockiest, furriest gorillas.

*White Nile*

*Horn of Africa*

*Congo*

*Great Rift Valley*

## Using tools
Gorillas and bonobos mainly eat plants and fruit, but chimpanzees are more carnivorous, and even use tools to help catch prey or collect food. They use twigs to pull termites from holes, sharpened sticks to spear tiny primates, and stones or clubs to crack nuts. Young chimpanzees watch older ones to learn how it is done.

## Threat display
Adult male gorillas intimidate rivals by standing upright to look bigger, while rhythmically beating their chest with cupped hands and hooting or roaring loudly. Older males are known as silverbacks.

**Male eastern mountain gorilla**

## Bonobo
Also called the pygmy chimpanzee, the bonobo is more lightly built than the chimpanzee. Its range is separated from that of its bigger cousins, who live on the other side of the great Congo River.

*Congo*

## Shrinking habitats
The chimpanzee has the widest range of any great ape and can survive in drier, more open woodland than bonobos and gorillas. But all great ape species are threatened with extinction as the cutting down of rainforest continues to shrink their natural habitats, while poaching kills large numbers every year.

**Tapanuli orangutan**
Only recently discovered in the rugged Tapanuli region, this rare ape was described as a separate species in 2017. Illegal hunting and tree-felling have left very few adult individuals.

MALAYSIA

**Baby orangutan**
An orangutan spends more time with its mother than almost any other animal. A baby clings to its mother for its first year, but even after seven years, youngsters may still seek their mother's protection.

**Sumatran orangutan**
The Sumatran orangutan has a cinnamon-coloured, long, fleecy, coat. Logging and plantations have pushed them up to the north of the island, and babies are caught for the illegal pet trade.

INDONESIA

Sumatra

Barisan Mountains

INDIAN OCEAN

**20%**
OF WILD ORANGUTANS **LIVE IN PROTECTED AREAS**

**Tree living**
Orangutans spend more time in the branches than the great apes of Africa (see pp.124–125). In the trees, they eat mainly fruit and leaves, and only rarely descend to the ground. They are also less sociable than chimpanzees and gorillas, except when breeding and raising young.

Sumatran orangutans

UP TO **3,000** BORNEAN ORANGUTANS **ARE KILLED** BY HUMANS **EVERY YEAR**

**Island refuges**
Orangutans once used to range across mainland Southeast Asia, but today they are only found in a few areas on the islands of Sumatra and Borneo in Indonesia.

**KEY**
◼ Sumatran orangutan
◼ Tapanuli orangutan
◼ Bornean orangutan

# Orangutans

Three species of orangutan represent the great apes of tropical Asia. They depend on their wild rainforest habitats, so are now endangered as deforestation breaks up their home ranges into ever smaller patches.

**Far from their kind**
Shrinking habitats, separated by barriers such as rivers or roads, make it harder for adult orangutans to meet and breed. This means fewer babies are born, and populations shrink.

**Fur colour**
Adult Bornean orangutans have orange-brown or maroon fur.

Borneo

**Bornean orangutan**
Mature male orangutans look very different from smaller females: males have fleshy cheek pads that stick out from the face, especially in the Bornean species.

**Under threat**
Sumatra and Borneo have lost more than half of their rainforests in the past century – mainly as trees are cleared for plantations that produce crops such as palm oil. If current trends continue, all orangutans could be extinct within decades.

Java

# Indian flying fox

With more than 1,400 species, bats make up the second-biggest order of mammals after the rodents, and live in most parts of the world except the poles and remote islands. The Indian flying fox is one of the world's largest bats, and is found in tropical forests and swamps across the Indian subcontinent.

THE **LARGEST-KNOWN ROOST** OF INDIAN FLYING FOXES WAS MADE UP OF **24,000 BATS**

**PAKISTAN**

**INDIA**

Narmada

Ganges

Godavari

Krishna

**Dry areas**
In the drier, eastern parts of their range, Indian flying foxes often live close to humans, where they can easily find sources of fruit and water on agricultural land.

**Mountain range**
Ranging into the foothills of the Himalayas, the Indian flying fox reaches altitudes of up to 2,000 m (6,560 ft). Here the bats have longer hair to survive the cooler highland climate.

**Helping trees**
As flying foxes cover long distances, they carry with them pollen from flowers, and also spread seeds that catch in their fur. This helps many forest trees to reproduce.

**Protected**
In some areas of its range, this bat is treated as a pest for eating farmers' fruit, but in southern India it is considered sacred and is protected.

**Long-lived roosts**
After night-time foraging, bats return to their roost at dawn to sleep. A colony can contain thousands of bats and may occupy the same location over generations. One roosting site in southern India was used for more than 75 years.

**KEY**
Indian flying fox range

**Forest colonies**
In Bangladesh, the biggest colonies of Indian flying foxes live in the densest forest – where there is a richer supply of fruiting trees and less disturbance from humans.

*Himalayas*

**Handy wing**
The wings of all bats are made of thin sheets of skin that extend out from the sides of the body and stretch between the long finger bones of their hands.

## Finding fruit

The Indian flying fox lives across India, Pakistan, Bangladesh, and Sri Lanka. These large, fruit-eating bats sleep through the day and wake at dusk to seek out food. They are known to fly up to 150 km (90 miles) in search of the best sources of food – especially fig trees that are heavy with fruit – which they locate with their highly sophisticated senses of sight and smell.

THE **WINGSPANS** OF INDIAN FLYING FOXES CAN REACH **UP TO 2 M** (6 FT)

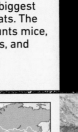

## OTHER BATS

**Ghost bat**
Northern Australia is home to one of the world's biggest predatory bats. The ghost bat hunts mice, lizards, birds, and other bats.

**Greater horseshoe bat**
Like many other bats, this species tracks insects in flight by homing in on the sound of echoed clicks. This is called echolocation.

**New Zealand lesser short-tailed bat**
Having evolved on islands originally free of predators, this bat crawls along the ground more than any other species.

**Madagascar sucker-footed bat**
This bat clings to the smooth surfaces in between folds of palm leaves using tiny suckers on its wrists and ankles.

**White-winged vampire bat**
This tropical South American bat mainly targets birds – biting and lapping the blood of a sleeping victim.

ASIA

Himalayas

**KEY**

☐ Tiger range

**ANIMALS IN DANGER**

**Tiger**
⚠ IUCN status: endangered
⊕ Population estimate: 2,150–3,160

**Bengal tigers**
On India's central plateau, below the Himalayas, Bengal tigers live in floodplains with marshes and oxbow lakes, as well as in the drier deciduous forest further south.

INDIA

**Dry and wet forests**
In southern India, Bengal tigers are found in the wet evergreen and dry deciduous forests in the hills that line the foothills of the Western Ghats.

**Mangrove habitat**
In far eastern India and Bangladesh, Bengal tigers cope with the changes of the coastal Sundarbans – the world's biggest area of mangrove forest, a place that is flooded daily by the tides.

INDIAN OCEAN

**Vanishing tigers**
A century ago, tigers lived from the Caspian Sea in the west to Java and Bali in the east. Today no tigers survive in these places, and throughout the rest of their range they exist in ever smaller patches. Poaching, often for the illegal trade in body parts which are used in traditional medicine, pose the biggest threat to remaining tigers.

Caspian Sea

RUSSIA

KAZAKHSTAN

CHINA

INDIA

INDONESIA

Java Bali

☐ Historic range

INDONESIA

**Indochinese tigers**
Tigers from the tropical rainforests and dry forests of mainland Southeast Asia are smaller than those of India but larger than the ones in Sumatra. Only a few hundred remain.

**Sumatran tigers**
The smallest tigers – nearly half the size of those from Siberia – live in the remaining rainforests of Sumatra in Indonesia. Their thinner coats are darker orange and have more stripes.

THERE ARE **MORE** TIGERS KEPT **IN CAPTIVITY** THAN THERE ARE IN THE **WILD**

A TIGER CAN **EAT** MORE THAN **35 KG (80 LB)** OF MEAT IN **ONE MEAL**

CHINA

## Siberian tigers
Tigers of Russia's Siberian pine forests are among the largest of all cats, with paler colouring, fewer stripes, and thick fur that keeps out the bitter cold of winter.

## Tiger territories
There are local populations of tigers in different regions of Asia, but they all belong to the same species. Adult tigers only come together to mate and otherwise live alone, patrolling territories to protect their own supply of prey. Since prey is scarcer for Siberian tigers, they need to roam territories four times bigger than those of the Bengal tigers on the Indian subcontinent.

## Top cat
A tiger has massive forelimbs, needed to strike with enough strength to bring down large prey. Its fiery-coloured coat helps to conceal it in sun-dappled forests.

# Tiger

The tiger is the world's biggest cat. But this formidable hunter is also hunted: across Asia, tiger numbers are falling as more become victim to poachers, or lose their habitat to farming, logging, and ever greater numbers of humans needing space.

## Lone hunter
Adult tigers hunt alone, stalking their prey from the cover of vegetation. Blending in, a tiger can sneak close to its prey before ambushing it. Grabbing the prey with its broad forepaws, and with its long claws extended, the tiger kills its victim by a bite to the neck.

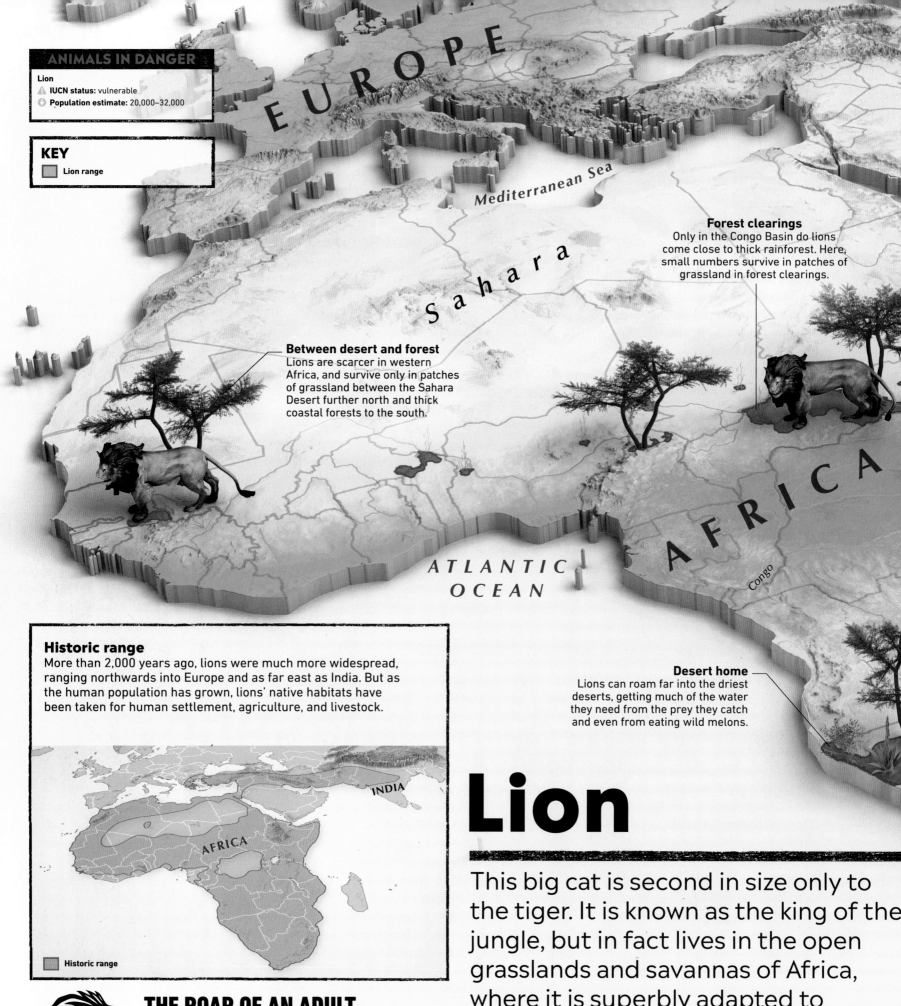

EUROPE

Mediterranean Sea

Sahara

ATLANTIC OCEAN

AFRICA

Congo

**Forest clearings**
Only in the Congo Basin do lions come close to thick rainforest. Here, small numbers survive in patches of grassland in forest clearings.

**Between desert and forest**
Lions are scarcer in western Africa, and survive only in patches of grassland between the Sahara Desert further north and thick coastal forests to the south.

**Desert home**
Lions can roam far into the driest deserts, getting much of the water they need from the prey they catch and even from eating wild melons.

**Historic range**
More than 2,000 years ago, lions were much more widespread, ranging northwards into Europe and as far east as India. But as the human population has grown, lions' native habitats have been taken for human settlement, agriculture, and livestock.

INDIA

AFRICA

▢ Historic range

# Lion

This big cat is second in size only to the tiger. It is known as the king of the jungle, but in fact lives in the open grasslands and savannas of Africa, where it is superbly adapted to hunting. Unlike most cats, which are solitary hunters, lions work together as a group, or pride, to bring down prey.

**THE ROAR OF AN ADULT MALE LION** IS SO LOUD THAT IT CAN BE HEARD CLEARLY UP TO **8 KM** (5 MILES) **AWAY**

# ASIA

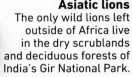

INDIA

**Asiatic lions**
The only wild lions left outside of Africa live in the dry scrublands and deciduous forests of India's Gir National Park.

**Savanna trees**
Although lions hunt in open grassland, a pride often gathers under shady trees during the heat of the day and climbs into branches to reach cool breezes. This vantage point also helps them spot prey animals travelling through the grasslands.

*Horn of Africa*

# Fragmented habitats

Lions once freely roamed the savannas, grasslands, scrub, and open woodlands of the African continent, but much of their natural habitat has been lost. They are now largely limited to game reserves and national parks.

**Mane**
The thicker and darker a male lion's mane is, the more attractive he is to females.

**Male lion**

*INDIAN OCEAN*

*Kalahari Desert*

*Namib Desert*

**Camouflage**
By matching the colour of the surrounding grassland of the African savanna, females can get close to prey – including targets as big as buffalo and giraffe – before giving chase.

**Retractable claws**
Like those of all cats, the long claws of a lion are pulled back when not in use. They are only extended when needed – such as for attacking prey.

**Female lion**

### Stealthy lynx

Recognizable by the pointy tufts of hair on their ears, these Iberian lynxes are hunting European rabbit – their favourite prey. Once common across the Iberian Peninsula, these cats are now found in only two small areas in southern Spain. A drop in rabbit populations and the spread of human settlements have led to their decline.

**NORTH AMERICA**

**SOUTH AMERICA**

**EUROPE**

**AFRICA**

**Finding prey**
Wolves from North America live in plains and forests where there is plenty of prey, including beavers, white-tailed deer, and moose. Packs work as a team when hunting big prey, but they hunt alone for smaller meals.

**Arctic tundra**
Arctic wolves are especially adapted to survive in the far-north regions of Greenland and North America.

**Local populations**
In different parts of the wolf's huge range, local populations have habitat-specific adaptations and even look different, from the northern Arctic wolf to the southern dingo. Butthey all belong to the same species – grey wolf. Packs control and hunt in vast territories, and they communicate with each other by howling and scent-marking.

**Padded feet**
The feet of wolves and dogs have soles with protective pads and clawed toes. Unlike those of cats, their claws are blunt and not retractable.

**Fur**
In most wolves the fur is mottled grey, but some wolves are born white or black. Wolves living in the coldest climates grow thicker fur.

# Grey wolf

This wide-ranging canine is a highly social animal, living and hunting in family groups, known as packs. It is found across vast areas of the globe in many different habitats, from the frozen Arctic to hot, dry deserts.

**Eurasian wolf**
Wolves that live in the forests of Scandinavia and Russia prey on anything from red deer and wild boar to hares and voles. They may also attack livestock and raid human garbage.

ASIA

**Himalayan habitat**
Found in a variety of alpine habitats, from high-altitude mountains to temperate forests, wolves living here hunt yaks and goats and shelter in alpine caves.

**Siberian tundra**
Living on the open frozen ground across northern Siberia, the large tundra wolf develops a thicker, darker coat in winter and hunts some of the largest prey, including caribou and musk ox.

**KEY**
Wolf range

**Dingo**
Dingoes are highly adaptable and can be found in every habitat in Australia, even deserts – as long as they have access to drinking water.

AUSTRALIA

**Australian dingoes**
All domesticated dogs, which we keep as pets, are descended from the grey wolf and belong to the same species. Dingoes originated from domesticated dogs that were brought to Australia from Asia by humans 4,000 years ago and then returned to the wild.

**Arctic wolves**
Found in the Arctic tundras of Greenland and North America, the Arctic wolf is one of the biggest types of wolf. It survives freezing conditions by having long thick fur and a thick layer of body fat, and stays white throughout the year as effective camouflage against the snow.

SOME WOLF **TERRITORIES** EXTEND UP TO **2,600 SQ KM** (1,000 SQ MILES)

THE **LARGEST-KNOWN PACK** WAS MADE UP OF **36** WOLVES

WOLVES CAN **ROAM** UP TO **30 KM** (12 MILES) IN A **SINGLE DAY**

**Brown bear**
Spanning the northern hemisphere, brown bears have the widest range of any bear species. On the Pacific coast of North America, they fish for salmon.

**Andean bear**
This shy bear is mainly a plant-eater. It prefers the remote rainforests of the Andes Mountains, though it will descend in search of food and has been found in many different habitats, including thorny dry forests and even coastal deserts.

**American black bear**
The most populous bear species is an excellent opportunist, eating seasonal nuts and berries, scavenging carrion, and even raiding human garbage or stores of food.

**Polar bear**
This bear eats meat and little else. It specializes in hunting for Arctic seals, and regularly swims more than 50 km (30 miles) in search of food.

**Grizzly bear**
The fur of brown bears varies in colour across their range. Some regional populations in North America have silver-tipped, or grizzly, hair.

NORTH AMERICA

SOUTH AMERICA

Greenland

EUROPE

AFRICA

## ANIMALS IN DANGER

**Andean bear**
⚠ **IUCN status:** vulnerable
◆ **Population estimate:** 2,500–10,000

**Polar bear**
⚠ **IUCN status:** vulnerable
◆ **Population estimate:** 22,000–31,000

**Sloth bear**
⚠ **IUCN status:** vulnerable
◆ **Population estimate:** unknown

## Range of habitats
Bears are found across Europe, Asia, North America, and in parts of South America. The largest bear species – polar and brown bears – live in the cold north. Further south, smaller bears with smaller ranges live in the tropics.

## Adapting to climate
Polar bears are perfectly adapted to life in their Arctic habitat. Their thick fur is made of hollow hairs that trap warmth close to the body. Even their paw pads are furry, with tiny bumps to help grip slippery ice. Their small ears and tail minimize heat loss. Loss of their unique habitat is putting these bears at risk, as climate change reduces the sea ice on which they depend.

**Brown bear**

# Bears

There are eight different species of bear across the world. They include the largest land carnivores with the power to bring down the biggest prey. But not all bears are ferocious hunters – some eat mainly insects, while others prefer plants and berries.

ASIA

**Asiatic black bear**
The Asiatic black bear lives in oak and beech forests where there are plenty of nuts and berries. It also feeds on fruit and occasionally hunts small mammals.

**Sloth bear**
In tropical Asia, the sloth bear has a fondness for ants, termites, and fruit. It lives in tropical lowland forests and occasionally can be found in tall grasslands.

**Giant panda**
Living in bamboo forests in the mountains of central China, this bear lives almost entirely on bamboo. Loss of their habitat means they are restricted to a very small area.

**Sun bear**
The smallest bear with the shortest coat lives in tropical forests, where it climbs trees for fruit, insects, and honey.

**Different diets**
Most bears are omnivorous – which means they eat both meat and plants. Some bears will eat anything available, while others are specialists that slurp insects or crunch bamboo. The sun bear uses its 25-cm- (10-in-) long tongue to lick up ants from logs.

## KEY

- ▢ Brown bear
- ▢ Andean bear
- ▢ American black bear
- ▢ Polar bear
- ▢ Sloth bear
- ▢ Sun bear
- ▢ Giant panda
- ▢ Asiatic black bear

**POLAR BEARS** ARE THE **BIGGEST SPECIES** AND CAN WEIGH **UP TO 800 KG** (1,760 LB)

THERE ARE FEWER THAN **2,000** **GIANT PANDAS** LEFT IN THE WILD

**HONEY BADGERS** CAN **STUN BEES** WITH A SQUIRT OF **REPELLENT** SPRAY FROM **GLANDS** AROUND THEIR **BOTTOM**

**HONEY BADGERS** ARE **RESISTANT** TO **SNAKE VENOM**

Sahara

Congo Basin

AFRICA

**Desert scavengers**
Along the fringes of the Sahara Desert, honey badgers are expert at digging out spiny-tailed lizards and gerbils from burrows, or grubbing for roots and insects, but they also scavenge on carrion (the flesh of dead animals).

**Helpful hunters**
In the grasslands of East Africa, other predators, such as goshawks and jackals, have learned to follow digging honey badgers, and catch small animals that escape their notice.

**Finding honey**
In central Africa, honey badgers roam in lush tropical rainforests, raiding wild bee hives to steal the honey, as well as to eat the bee larvae.

**Thick-skinned badger**
The honey badger's thick skin is loose, especially around the neck, enabling it to twist around to bite when grabbed by an attacker. A thick skin also protects it from snake bites and bee stings.

**Badger baby**
Honey badger mothers bring up their babies alone, moving them from den to den in their mouth every few days.

**Fearless badgers**
Sometimes honey badgers see off threats from predators much larger than themselves, such as this pack of wild dogs. Although they will rarely pick a fight, if attacked they rush at the assailants, hissing, raising their hackles, and releasing a stench from their anal glands.

**KEY**

☐ Honey badger range

**Caspian badgers**
On the dry, grassy plains of southwest Asia, the honey badger reaches the northernmost limits of its range around the Caspian Sea.

Caspian Sea

ASIA

Arabian Peninsula

INDIA

**Arabian badgers**
Honey badgers survive the dry deserts of the Arabian Peninsula by catching venomous prey, including scorpions and snakes. They shelter under rocks during the hottest part of the day.

**Indian badgers**
The honey badger is widespread across the Indian subcontinent, but is most common in forests and grasslands, where it may share its territory with tigers and sloth bears.

## Opportunistic living

Few animals can survive such a wide range of habitats as the honey badger. Across Africa, India, and the Arabian Peninsula, it lives in forests, savanna, marshes, and deserts – wherever this nocturnal animal can dig a burrow. It is not found in the very driest parts of the Sahara.

# Honey badger

Six species of badgers live across North America, Africa, and Eurasia – and all are stocky, strong-bodied animals. The honey badger has a particular reputation for toughness. With a strong bite, thick skin, and sharp claws, it is a fierce hunter that braves stinging bees to satisfy its taste for honey.

**Digging for prey**
As well as excavating burrows, the strong front paws with their long claws can rip open bee hives and dig out animal prey such as rodents from underground. Food is found by smell and sound.

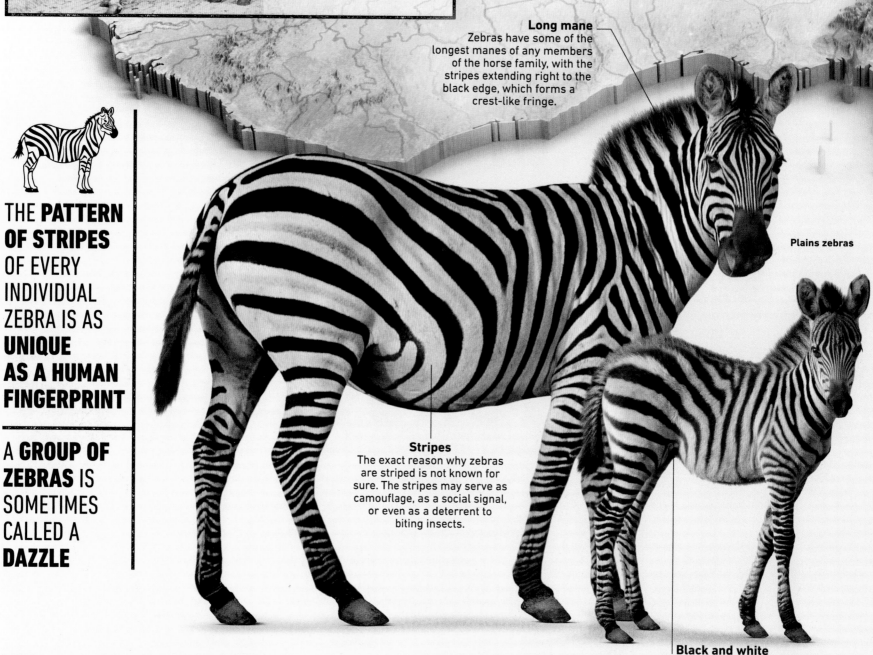

## Quagga

A subspecies of the plains zebra with fewer stripes, called the quagga, was once common in southern Africa, but was hunted to extinction by about 1883. Today scientists are breeding zebra with quagga-like characteristics to try to bring the animal back.

## African grazers

Zebras graze on the grasses of a variety of habitats, from the plains zebra in open grasslands and savannas, to the Grevy's zebra in semi-arid scrub, and the mountain zebra on mountainous slopes and plateaus. During the dry season, the Grevy's and mountain zebras spread out further in their range to find better sources of food and water, but the plains zebra follows seasonal rains – to wherever the grass is greener – in large migrations.

**Long mane**
Zebras have some of the longest manes of any members of the horse family, with the stripes extending right to the black edge, which forms a crest-like fringe.

**Plains zebras**

THE **PATTERN OF STRIPES** OF EVERY INDIVIDUAL ZEBRA IS AS **UNIQUE AS A HUMAN FINGERPRINT**

A **GROUP OF ZEBRAS** IS SOMETIMES CALLED A **DAZZLE**

**Stripes**
The exact reason why zebras are striped is not known for sure. The stripes may serve as camouflage, as a social signal, or even as a deterrent to biting insects.

**Black and white**
Underneath their fur, zebras actually have dark skin. Their stripes develop as white over black rather than vice versa.

# Zebras

Zebras are the most distinctive members of the horse family. Three species live on the grassy savannas in the eastern and southern parts of Africa, each with their own species-specific pattern of stripes.

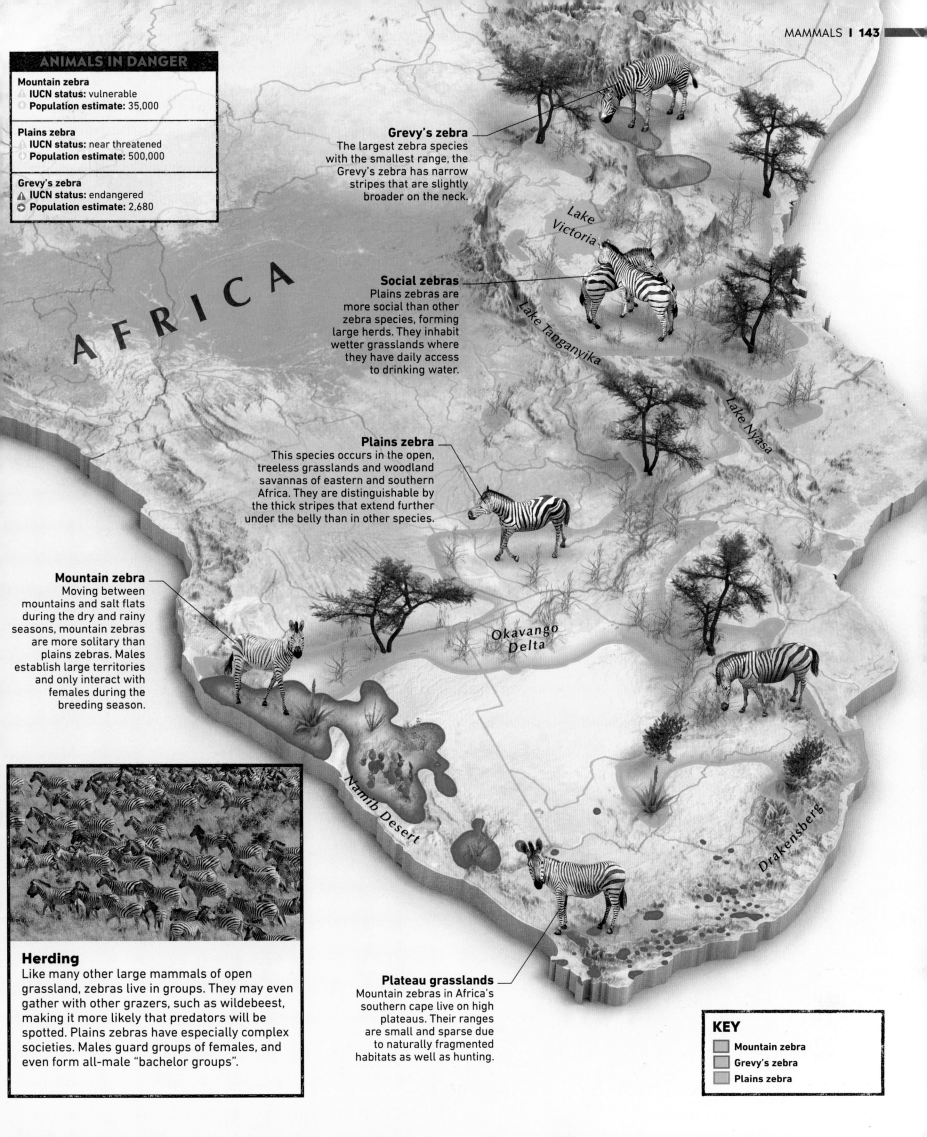

## ANIMALS IN DANGER

**Mountain zebra**
⚠ **IUCN status:** vulnerable
◇ **Population estimate:** 35,000

**Plains zebra**
⚠ **IUCN status:** near threatened
◇ **Population estimate:** 500,000

**Grevy's zebra**
⚠ **IUCN status:** endangered
◇ **Population estimate:** 2,680

AFRICA

### Grevy's zebra
The largest zebra species with the smallest range, the Grevy's zebra has narrow stripes that are slightly broader on the neck.

Lake Victoria

Lake Tanganyika

Lake Nyasa

### Social zebras
Plains zebras are more social than other zebra species, forming large herds. They inhabit wetter grasslands where they have daily access to drinking water.

### Plains zebra
This species occurs in the open, treeless grasslands and woodland savannas of eastern and southern Africa. They are distinguishable by the thick stripes that extend further under the belly than in other species.

### Mountain zebra
Moving between mountains and salt flats during the dry and rainy seasons, mountain zebras are more solitary than plains zebras. Males establish large territories and only interact with females during the breeding season.

Okavango Delta

Namib Desert

Drakensberg

## Herding
Like many other large mammals of open grassland, zebras live in groups. They may even gather with other grazers, such as wildebeest, making it more likely that predators will be spotted. Plains zebras have especially complex societies. Males guard groups of females, and even form all-male "bachelor groups".

### Plateau grasslands
Mountain zebras in Africa's southern cape live on high plateaus. Their ranges are small and sparse due to naturally fragmented habitats as well as hunting.

### KEY
■ Mountain zebra
■ Grevy's zebra
■ Plains zebra

THE ESTIMATED **NUMBER** LEFT OF ADULT BREEDING **JAVAN RHINOS IS ONLY** 18

RHINOS ARE **HUNTED FOR** THEIR **HORNS**, WHICH ARE WORTH MORE THAN THEIR **WEIGHT IN GOLD**

*ATLANTIC OCEAN*

AFRICA

**Black rhinoceros**
Just four countries – Kenya, Zimbabwe, Namibia, and South Africa – protect more than 95 per cent of all surviving black rhinoceroses. Protection means that numbers are rising in these nations.

**White rhinoceros**
Most remaining white rhinos are found in the grasslands of southern Africa; a few have been reintroduced to eastern parts of the continent.

KENYA

TANZANIA

ANGOLA

ZAMBIA

NAMIBIA

BOTSWANA

ZIMBABWE

MOZAMBIQUE

SOUTH AFRICA

**Black and white**
Despite their names, both kinds of African rhinoceroses are in fact greyish-brown. These symbols are black or white to distinguish the two species on the map.

**Thick-skinned**
The black rhino has coarse skin, in places up to 4 cm (1½ in) thick. This protects it from being scratched by thorny shrubs as it eats.

**Mud bath**
All rhinoceroses, including this female black rhino and her calf, like to wallow in mud pools. It helps to cool the body and protect it from biting insects.

**Grasping lip**
The finger-like upper lip of the black rhino helps to grasp foliage. White rhinos have a flat, wide upper lip for grazing grass.

**Black rhinoceros**

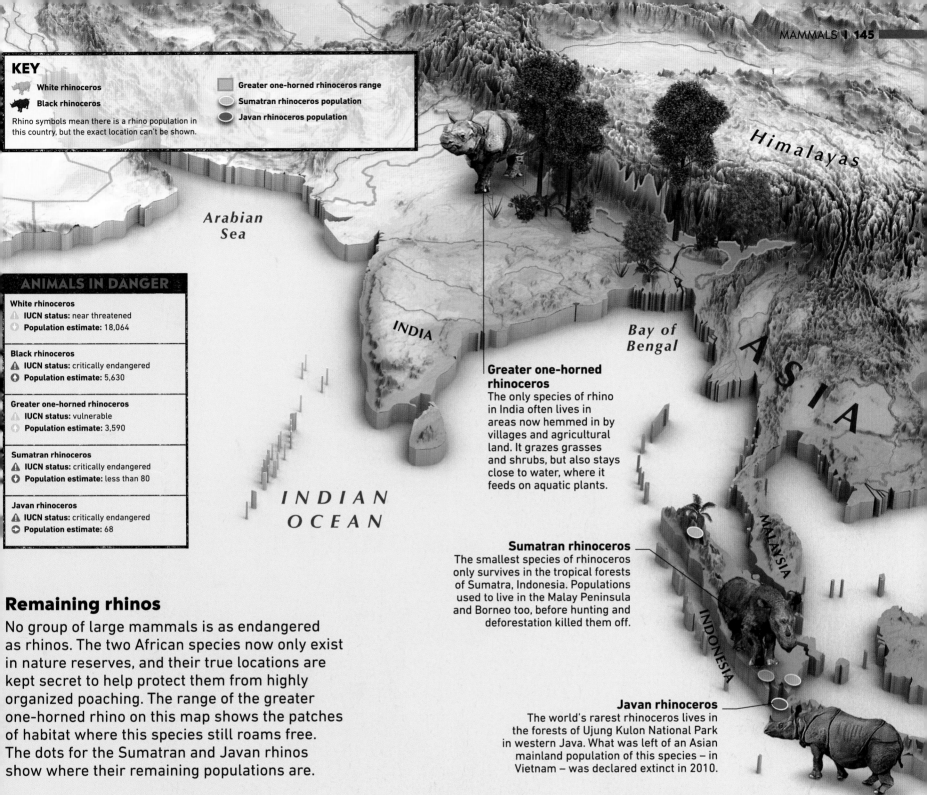

## KEY

🦏 White rhinoceros

🦏 Black rhinoceros

Rhino symbols mean there is a rhino population in this country, but the exact location can't be shown.

⬜ Greater one-horned rhinoceros range

⬭ Sumatran rhinoceros population

⬤ Javan rhinoceros population

### ANIMALS IN DANGER

**White rhinoceros**
⚠ IUCN status: near threatened
🔾 Population estimate: 18,064

**Black rhinoceros**
⚠ IUCN status: critically endangered
🔾 Population estimate: 5,630

**Greater one-horned rhinoceros**
⚠ IUCN status: vulnerable
🔾 Population estimate: 3,590

**Sumatran rhinoceros**
⚠ IUCN status: critically endangered
🔾 Population estimate: less than 80

**Javan rhinoceros**
⚠ IUCN status: critically endangered
🔾 Population estimate: 68

*Arabian Sea*

*Himalayas*

INDIA

*Bay of Bengal*

A S I A

MALAYSIA

INDONESIA

INDIAN OCEAN

### Greater one-horned rhinoceros

The only species of rhino in India often lives in areas now hemmed in by villages and agricultural land. It grazes grasses and shrubs, but also stays close to water, where it feeds on aquatic plants.

### Sumatran rhinoceros

The smallest species of rhinoceros only survives in the tropical forests of Sumatra, Indonesia. Populations used to live in the Malay Peninsula and Borneo too, before hunting and deforestation killed them off.

### Javan rhinoceros

The world's rarest rhinoceros lives in the forests of Ujung Kulon National Park in western Java. What was left of an Asian mainland population of this species – in Vietnam – was declared extinct in 2010.

## Remaining rhinos

No group of large mammals is as endangered as rhinos. The two African species now only exist in nature reserves, and their true locations are kept secret to help protect them from highly organized poaching. The range of the greater one-horned rhino on this map shows the patches of habitat where this species still roams free. The dots for the Sumatran and Javan rhinos show where their remaining populations are.

# Rhinos

In prehistoric times, rhinoceroses ranged across large areas of the globe. Today, five species survive on savannas in Africa and in forests and grassland in Asia, but poaching and habitat destruction have edged these unique creatures to the brink of extinction.

### Guarded treasure

Rhinos are poached for their horns, which some people wrongly believe have medicinal qualities. Armed guards help protect some rhinos, including this white rhino in Kenya.

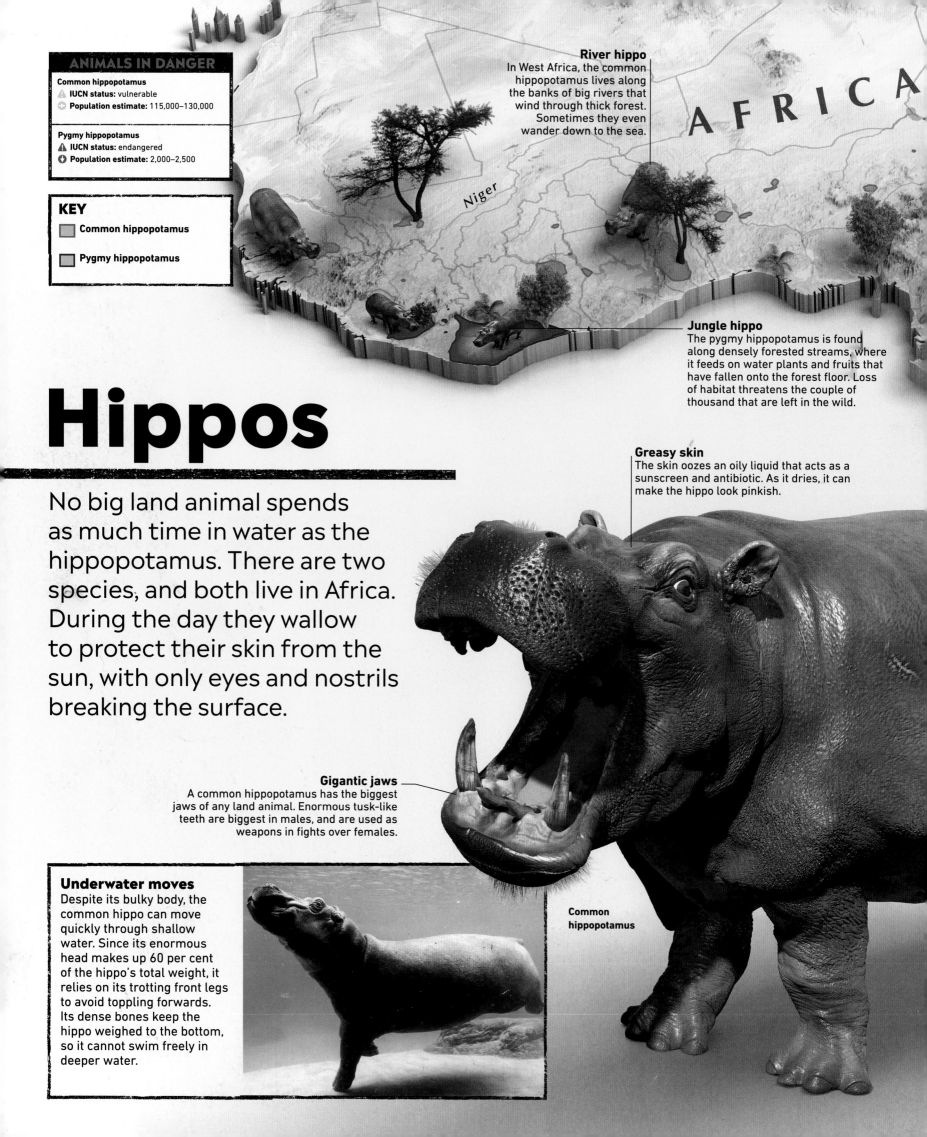

# Hippos

AFRICA

Niger

**River hippo**
In West Africa, the common hippopotamus lives along the banks of big rivers that wind through thick forest. Sometimes they even wander down to the sea.

**Jungle hippo**
The pygmy hippopotamus is found along densely forested streams, where it feeds on water plants and fruits that have fallen onto the forest floor. Loss of habitat threatens the couple of thousand that are left in the wild.

**Greasy skin**
The skin oozes an oily liquid that acts as a sunscreen and antibiotic. As it dries, it can make the hippo look pinkish.

No big land animal spends as much time in water as the hippopotamus. There are two species, and both live in Africa. During the day they wallow to protect their skin from the sun, with only eyes and nostrils breaking the surface.

**Gigantic jaws**
A common hippopotamus has the biggest jaws of any land animal. Enormous tusk-like teeth are biggest in males, and are used as weapons in fights over females.

**Underwater moves**
Despite its bulky body, the common hippo can move quickly through shallow water. Since its enormous head makes up 60 per cent of the hippo's total weight, it relies on its trotting front legs to avoid toppling forwards. Its dense bones keep the hippo weighed to the bottom, so it cannot swim freely in deeper water.

**Common hippopotamus**

**Fertile lakes**
Dung produced by hundreds of pooping hippos helps to enrich lakes, fertilizing the water with nutrients that can support food chains with big shoals of fishes.

Lake Victoria

Lake Tanganyika

Congo

Okavango Delta

Namib Desert

**Coastal hippos**
The coast of the Namib Desert is the only place where hippos can be seen cooling off in shallow seawater.

A HIPPO CAN **OPEN ITS** ENORMOUS MOUTH UP TO AN ANGLE OF

# 180

**DEGREES –** WIDER THAN ANY OTHER **LARGE MAMMAL**

**ADULT MALE** COMMON HIPPOS CAN WEIGH UP TO **2,000 KG** (4,400 LB)

**Nocturnal grazer**
The common hippo gets most of its food on land. It grazes on grass at night, using its fleshy lips to pluck the blades.

## Hippo havens

The common hippopotamus, the larger of the two species, lives in patches of woodland and grassland around rivers across sub-Saharan Africa. The pygmy hippopotamus only survives in a few fragments of rainforest in West Africa.

HIPPOS CAN **HOLD THEIR BREATH** FOR **5 MINUTES** SUBMERGED **IN WATER**

**Mini hippo**
The forest-dwelling pygmy hippopotamus is about half as tall as its bigger cousin. Shaded by over-hanging trees, it probably spends more time out of water during the day than the common hippo, but its habits are little known.

 **KG** (1,700 LB) IS THE **HEAVIEST RECORDED WEIGHT** OF AN ADULT MALE MOOSE

**MOOSE ANTLERS** ARE MADE OF **BONE** – THEY ARE THE **FASTEST-GROWING BONES** IN THE ANIMAL KINGDOM

## Alaskan giants
The biggest moose occur in Alaska and Siberia. Calves born in Alaska can weigh nearly twice as much as those born in Europe.

**KEY**

Moose range

## Migration
In the parts of their range with the coldest winters – in North America and Siberia – moose migrate south during the bitter months in search of better food. North American moose may travel up to 200 km (125 miles).

## Antler
A male's antlers start growing in April and are fully formed by summer. Antlers are covered in a nourishing layer of skin, called velvet, that gets rubbed off before the antler is shed in December.

## Marshes and wetlands
Moose favour the damp, boreal forests that stretch across North America, Europe, and northern Asia, where the snow does not get too deep in winter and temperatures remain cool in summer. They stick to wetland areas, where their favourite food plants – birch, alder, and willow trees – grow in abundance.

# Moose

The world's biggest species of deer also has one of the widest ranges. The moose is an animal of marshy forests and is found across temperate regions of the northern hemisphere – where there is plenty of vegetation to browse and cover for females to raise their calves.

**Motherly care**
A female moose gives birth to one or two calves and feeds them with milk for up to five months. The thick cover of the northern forests helps to protect them from predatory grey wolves and brown bears.

**Bellowing bull**
During the breeding season, most male moose defend a female by bellowing loudly and thrashing the vegetation aggressively with their antlers to warn other males to stay away.

EUROPE

ASIA

**Mountain forests**
In Asia, moose are widespread throughout the forests of Siberia. They are found at their highest altitude in central Asia, including up to 1,700 m (5,580 ft) above sea level in the Altai Mountains.

**Shrinking range**
In prehistory, moose were found as far west as the British Isles and the Pyrenees. Hunting restricted them to Scandinavia and eastern Europe, but their numbers here have increased in the last 50 years. In Europe, moose are commonly known as elk.

**Northern tundra**
In the northernmost parts of their range – in the open Arctic tundra – food is scarcer and more scattered. Here, dominant males compete to mate with groups of females called harems.

**Giant antlers**
Like almost all other deer, only male moose grow antlers. These enormous bony weapons – each more than 1 m (3 ft) long – grow new each year as males defend their mates and territories, before being shed at the end of each breeding season.

AUSTRALIA

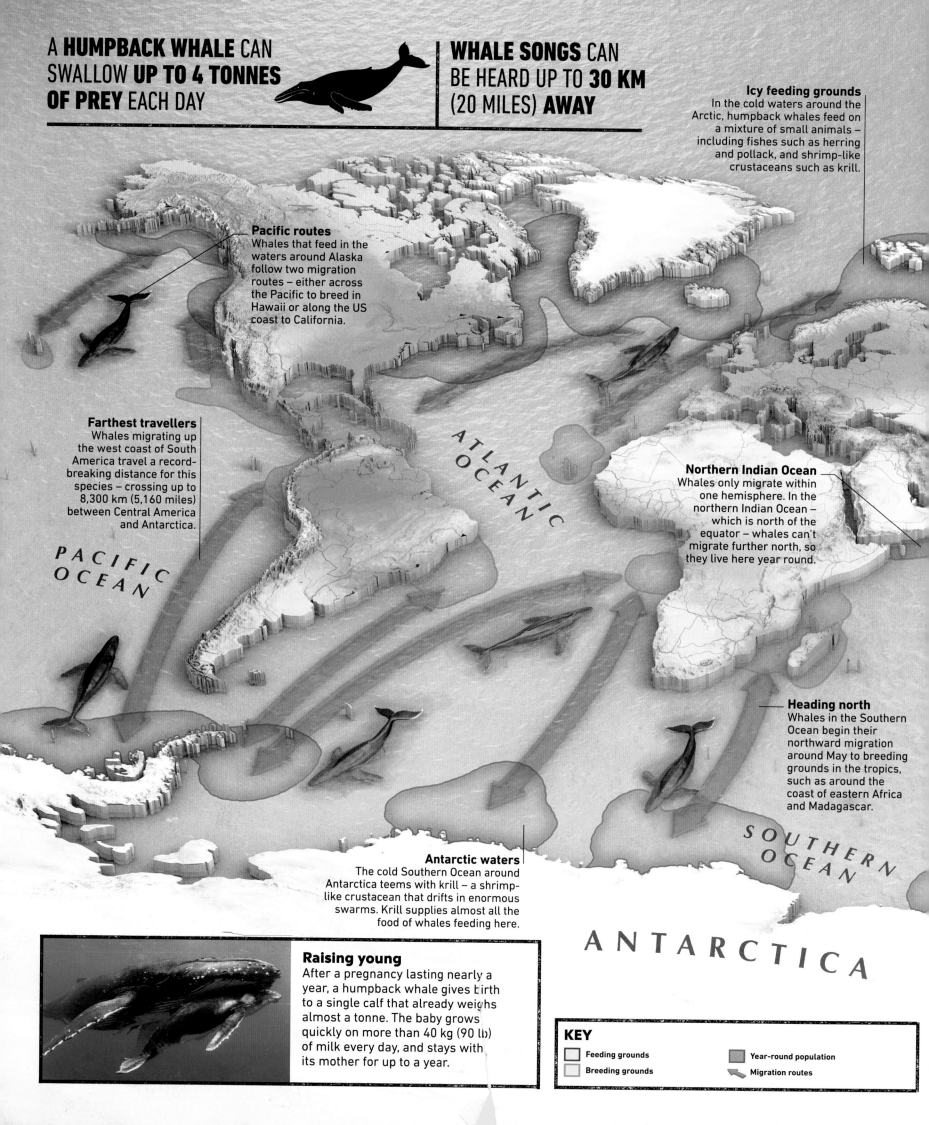

**A HUMPBACK WHALE CAN SWALLOW UP TO 4 TONNES OF PREY EACH DAY**

**WHALE SONGS CAN BE HEARD UP TO 30 KM (20 MILES) AWAY**

**Icy feeding grounds**
In the cold waters around the Arctic, humpback whales feed on a mixture of small animals – including fishes such as herring and pollack, and shrimp-like crustaceans such as krill.

**Pacific routes**
Whales that feed in the waters around Alaska follow two migration routes – either across the Pacific to breed in Hawaii or along the US coast to California.

**Farthest travellers**
Whales migrating up the west coast of South America travel a record-breaking distance for this species – crossing up to 8,300 km (5,160 miles) between Central America and Antarctica.

**Northern Indian Ocean**
Whales only migrate within one hemisphere. In the northern Indian Ocean – which is north of the equator – whales can't migrate further north, so they live here year round.

ATLANTIC OCEAN

PACIFIC OCEAN

**Heading north**
Whales in the Southern Ocean begin their northward migration around May to breeding grounds in the tropics, such as around the coast of eastern Africa and Madagascar.

SOUTHERN OCEAN

**Antarctic waters**
The cold Southern Ocean around Antarctica teems with krill – a shrimp-like crustacean that drifts in enormous swarms. Krill supplies almost all the food of whales feeding here.

ANTARCTICA

**Raising young**
After a pregnancy lasting nearly a year, a humpback whale gives birth to a single calf that already weighs almost a tonne. The baby grows quickly on more than 40 kg (90 lb) of milk every day, and stays with its mother for up to a year.

**KEY**
Feeding grounds
Breeding grounds
Year-round population
Migration routes

# Humpback whale

Along with dolphins and porpoises, whales are cetaceans – aquatic mammals that have evolved to swim in the oceans. Together with 14 other species, the humpback whale is a filter feeder – it gulps huge mouthfuls of water and strains out zooplankton (tiny drifting animals) and small swimming fishes.

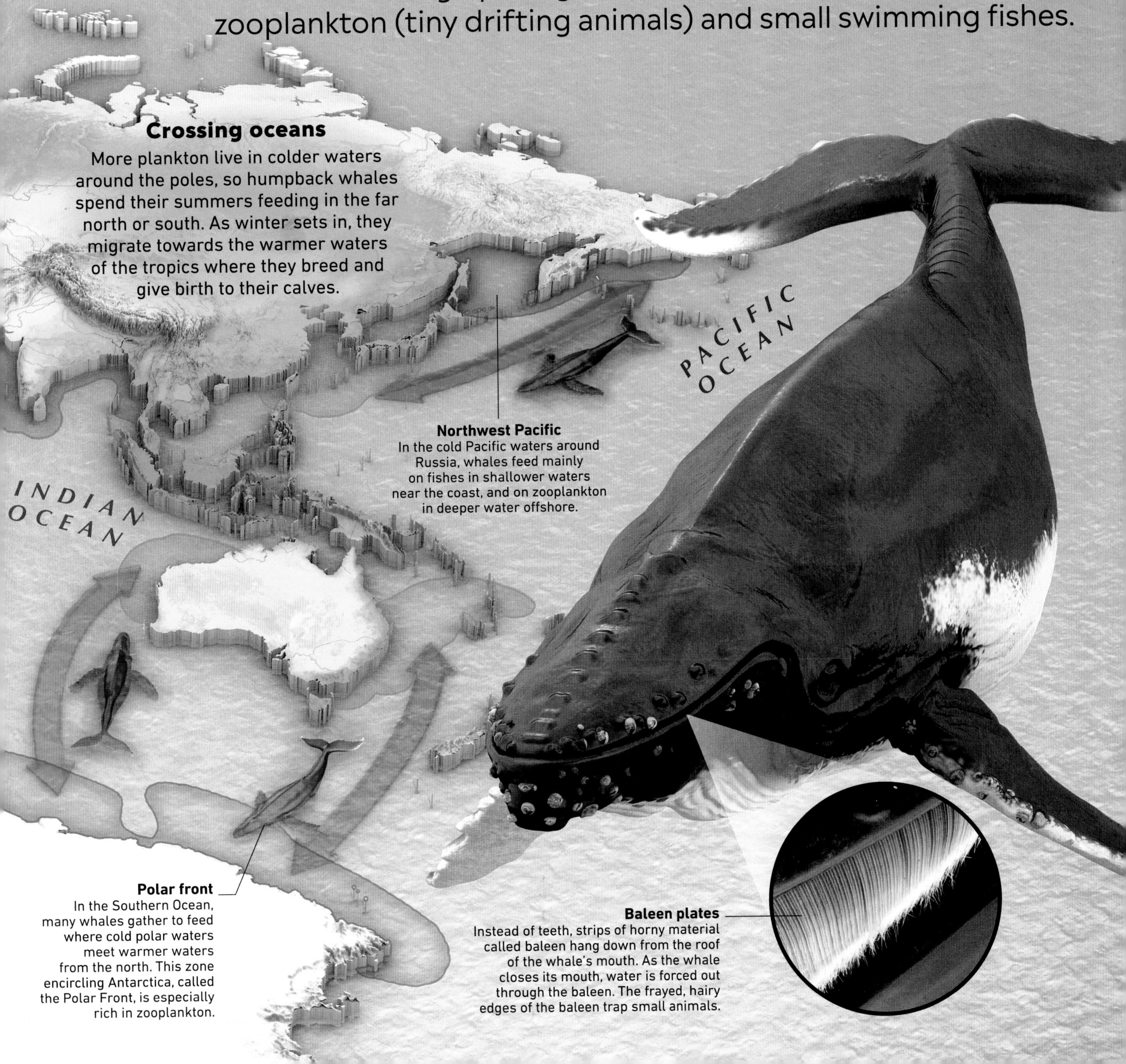

ARCTIC OCEAN

## Crossing oceans

More plankton live in colder waters around the poles, so humpback whales spend their summers feeding in the far north or south. As winter sets in, they migrate towards the warmer waters of the tropics where they breed and give birth to their calves.

PACIFIC OCEAN

### Northwest Pacific
In the cold Pacific waters around Russia, whales feed mainly on fishes in shallower waters near the coast, and on zooplankton in deeper water offshore.

INDIAN OCEAN

### Polar front
In the Southern Ocean, many whales gather to feed where cold polar waters meet warmer waters from the north. This zone encircling Antarctica, called the Polar Front, is especially rich in zooplankton.

### Baleen plates
Instead of teeth, strips of horny material called baleen hang down from the roof of the whale's mouth. As the whale closes its mouth, water is forced out through the baleen. The frayed, hairy edges of the baleen trap small animals.

### Unicorns of the sea
Related to whales and dolphins, the narwhal spends much of its time under the thick winter ice of the Arctic seas, only surfacing between ice sheets to breathe. Males grow a distinctive tusk up to 3 m (10 ft) long that is actually a long, sensitive tooth. The tusk is likely used to show dominance or during mating rituals.

# Glossary

**Adaptation**
The way in which a living species has evolved its appearance or behaviour, to fit in with its environment.

**Alpine**
Refers to something that lives or grows in mountainous areas.

**Aquatic**
Describes organisms that live in water.

**Arctic Circle**
The imaginary line that encircles the Arctic regions of Eurasia and North America.

**Biome**
A large area that has a particular climate, type of vegetation, and animals living in it.

**Browse**
Describes when animals feed on leaves and twigs from shrubs and trees, higher above ground.

**Bycatch**
Fish or other animals caught by mistake in nets laid out to catch other species.

**Canopy**
The topmost branches of the trees in a forest.

**Carnivorous**
Describes an animal that only eats meat.

**Carrion**
The remains of dead animals that scavengers feed on.

**Cartilage**
The tough, flexible material that makes up the skeleton of animals such as sharks.

**Climate**
The average weather conditions of an area over time.

**Climate change**
The process of gradual change to Earth's climate due to human activity.

**Cold-blooded**
Describes an animal whose body heat depends on the temperature of its surroundings, such as reptiles.

**Colony**
A group of animals – usually, but not always, of the same species – that live together.

**Coniferous**
A type of tree or shrub, such as pine, fir, or juniper, that has needles instead of leaves.

**Conservation**
The saving or protecting of animals or natural habitats.

**Continent**
One of the seven large landmasses on Earth: North America, South America, Europe, Africa, Asia, Australasia and Oceania, and Antarctica.

**Continental shelf**
The submerged edge of a continent that lies beneath shallow coastal seas.

**Coral reef**
A colony of corals growing in a rock-like formation on the seabed, home to a diverse range of marine life.

**Crustacean**
An animal with a hard external skeleton and paired, jointed legs, such as lobsters, crabs, and shrimps.

**Deciduous**
A type of tree, such as oak or birch, that loses leaves each year during a cold or dry season.

**Deforestation**
The cutting down of forests for timber or to clear land for farming or roads.

**Delta**
A low-lying, fan-shaped area at a river mouth, usually where the river flows into the sea.

**Domesticated**
Refers to an animal species that has been bred to be tamed and lives alongside people.

**Echinoderm**
One of a group of animals that includes spiny-skinned marine species, such as starfish and sea urchins.

**Endemic**
An animal or plant that is native to one specific area and found nowhere else.

**Equator**
An imaginary line, at 0° latitude, that divides Earth into the northern and southern hemispheres.

**Estuary**
The part of a river where it flows out into the sea, affected by tides.

**Evolution**
How animals and plants change over many generations as they survive and adapt.

**Exoskeleton**
The tough external skeleton of an animal such as an insect.

**Extinct**
Refers to an animal species that no longer exists because the last remaining individuals have died out.

**Fertilization**
The joining of male and female cells so they develop into seeds or a new organism. Also when dung or chemical fertilizers are spread on fields to make crops grow better.

**Gills**
The organ used by fish and other animals for breathing underwater.

**Glands**
Organs that produce hormones, or substances such as mucus, venom, or poison.

**Habitat**
The environment or place in which an animal normally lives.

**Hemisphere**
The northern hemisphere is the half of Earth north of the equator; the southern hemisphere is the half of the globe to the south of it.

**Hibernation**
When an animal hibernates, or goes into a deep, long sleep, to preserve energy during the cold season.

**Incubate**
To keep eggs warm so they can develop and hatch.

**Intertidal zone**
The part of the shore affected by tides. This area is covered by water when the tide comes in, and emerges when the tide goes out.

**Invertebrate**
An animal without a backbone, for example an insect, worm, or crustacean.

**Ivory**
The hard substance from which elephant tusks are made.

**Jet propulsion**
The act of pushing forwards by jetting out water, used by squids and octopuses.

**Keratin**
A tough material that makes up body parts such as hair, feathers, scales, and claws.

**Krill**
Tiny marine crustaceans that many animals, such as fish, whales, and seabirds, depend on for food.

**Larva**
The immature stage of animals that hatch from eggs and undergo metamorphosis (complete change) to become adults.

**Mangrove**
Trees that grow along muddy shores and river banks, often in salty water, and with many of their roots exposed.

**Marine**
Relating to the ocean or sea.

**Metamorphosis**
When an animal goes through a major change in body shape during its life cycle, such as when a caterpillar turns into a butterfly.

**Microscopic**
Something that is very small and can be seen only through a microscope.

**Migration**
The regular movement of animals from one place to another, often to find food or breed.

**Mimicry**
When an animal has evolved to look or act like another animal, in order to attract prey, or avoid getting eaten.

**Mollusc**
One of a group of invertebrates that includes snails, clams, and octopuses.

**Monotreme**
A group of mammals that lay eggs.

**Moult**
The way an animal sheds part of its outer skin, coat, or exoskeleton. In crustaceans, the regular shedding of the hard outer skeleton (exoskeleton) to allow the animal to grow.

**Nectar**
A sugar solution produced by flowers to attract pollinating animals such as bees and butterflies.

**Nocturnal**
When an animal is active at night.

**Nutrition**
The process of eating and processing food to absorb substances necessary for life.

**Omnivorous**
Refers to an animal that eats plants and meat.

**Oxbow lake**
A U-shaped lake formed from a river bend cut off from a river that over time has changed its course.

**Pampas**
Wide-stretching, grass-covered plains in temperate parts of South America.

**Parasite**
An organism that feeds on another, called the host, weakening it, and sometimes eventually killing it.

**Pesticide**
Chemicals used to kill insects and other pests that eat or damage crops.

**Pigment**
A substance that gives something colour.

**Plankton**
Small organisms that drift in water.

**Poaching**
Illegal hunting and killing of wild animals.

**Pollination**
When insects and other animals carry pollen from one flower to another so that fertilization takes place and new plants can grow.

**Prairie**
Large, flat grasslands, with very few trees, in North America.

**Prehensile**
Able to coil around an object and grip it, like the tail of a monkey or chameleon.

**Primate**
One of a group of animals that includes lemurs, monkeys, apes, and humans.

**Proboscis**
A long snout, or similar organ.

**Protein**
A type of complex chemical found in all living things.

**Range**
Referring to the territory, or area, within which an animal lives.

**River basin**
The land in which water gathers from one or more rivers.

**Roost**
To settle for the night, or a place where birds, bats, and butterflies do this.

**Savanna**
Open grasslands in tropical regions, with only a few trees.

**Scavenger**
An animal that feeds on the remains of dead animals or other organic waste from living organisms.

**Spawning**
Releasing eggs and sperm into water so that fertilization can take place.

**Species**
A group of similar organisms than can interbreed and produce fertile offspring.

**Subcontinent**
A large landmass that is part of a bigger continent.

**Subspecies**
A variant of a species, usually only found in one particular area.

**Subtropical**
An area or climate that is nearly tropical, located at the northern or southern edge of the tropics.

**Taiga**
The vast coniferous forests covering the northern parts of Eurasia and North America.

**Talons**
The large, hooked claws of a bird of prey.

**Temperate**
The mild, variable climate found in areas between the tropics and the cold polar regions.

**Thermals**
Currents of rising warm air.

**Tropical**
Referring to the climate or habitats in the region around the equator, known as the tropics.

**Tundra**
A treeless habitat in the cold, northernmost parts of North America, Europe, and Asia, in which the ground is frozen for much of the year.

# Index

# Acknowledgements

Dorling Kindersley would like to thank: Sheila Collins for design assistance; Georgina Palffy for editorial assistance; Hazel Beynon for proofreading; Elizabeth Wise for indexing.

**The publisher would like to thank the following for their kind permission to reproduce their photographs:**

(Key: a-above; b-below/bottom; c-centre; f-far; l-left; r-right; t-top)

**2 FLPA:** Greg Basco, BIA / Minden Pictures. **4 Alamy Stock Photo:** Narint Asawaphisith (crb). **Getty Images:** Martin Harvey / The Image Bank (tr); James L. Amos / Corbis Documentary (cr). **5 Alamy Stock Photo:** David Carillet (tr). **Dreamstime.com:** Toldiu74 (cl). **Getty Images:** jopstock (clb); Paul Starosta (tl). **6-7 FLPA:** Ralph Pace / Minden Pictures (b). **8-9 Getty Images:** Martin Harvey / The Image Bank. **10-11 Alamy Stock Photo:** National Geographic Image Collection (c). **12 Alamy Stock Photo:** Jelger Herder / Buiten-Beeld (tr); Val Duncan / Kenebec Images (cr); franzfoto.com (cb); Sheila Haddad / Danita Delimont (br); National Geographic Image Collection (tc). **naturepl.com:** Matthias Breiter (cla). **13 Alamy Stock Photo:** John Bennet (bc); Anatoliy Lastovetskiy (bl); Michal Sikorski (crb); Eric Dragesco / Nature Picture Library (cr). **14 Alamy Stock Photo:** Urbach, James / Superstock (c). **Dreamstime.com:** Svetlana Foote (crb). **naturepl.com:** Jane Burton (br). **15 Alamy Stock Photo:** Nobuo Matsumura (cr). **Getty Images:** uzairabdrahim (cra). **naturepl.com:** Cyril Ruoso (clb). **16 Dreamstime.com:** Sandamali Fernando (cra). **17 Alamy Stock Photo:** Ryhor Bruyeu (cl); Allen Galiza (tr). **Getty Images / iStock:** DaveThomasNZ (cr). **Getty Images:** Caroline Pang (bl); UniversalImagesGroup (tl). **18-19 Getty Images:** Ralph Lee Hopkins. **20 Getty Images:** Picture by Tambako the Jaguar. **21 Alamy Stock Photo:** Kevin Elsby (clb); Alex Mustard / Nature Picture Library (cla). **Getty Images:** Arterra (cr); Don Smith (tr); Michael Mike L. Baird flickr.bairdphotos.com (bl); Sandra Standbridge (br). **22-23 Getty Images:** James L. Amos / Corbis Documentary. **24 123RF.com:** Igor Serdiuk (bc); Anna Zakharchenko (c). **Richard E. Lee:** (crb). **Science Photo Library:** Woods Hole Oceanographic Institution, Visuals Unlimited (br). **25 Alamy Stock Photo:** Philip Dalton (br); Fiedler, W. / juniors@wildlife / Juniors Bildarchiv GmbH (tr). **naturepl.com:** Gavin Maxwell (cb). **26 naturepl.com:** Fred Bavendam (clb). **27 naturepl.com:** Fred Bavendam (tr). **28 naturepl.com:** Doug Perrine (bc). **29 Alamy Stock Photo:** Marevision / agefotostock (tr). **30 Dreamstime.com:** Cosmin Manci (tl). **30-31 Dreamstime.com:** Lee Amery (cb). **31 Dreamstime.com:** Maria Shchipakina (br). **Getty Images / iStock:** Merrimon (tr). **32-33 naturepl.com:** Phil Savoie. **34-35 Natural History Museum Bern,. 34 Alamy Stock Photo:** Razvan Cornel Constantin (br). **35 Alamy Stock Photo:** FLPA (bl). **36 Alamy Stock Photo:** FLPA (bl). **37 Alamy Stock Photo:** blickwinkel / H. Baesemann (br). **38-39 Alamy Stock Photo:** Narint Asawaphisith. **40 Alamy Stock Photo:** Jezper (bl). **naturepl.com:** Piotr Naskrecki (bc/ Lungfish). **Shutterstock.com:** Rachasie (bc). **41 Alamy Stock Photo:** blickwinkel / F. Teigler (c); WaterFrame_sta / :WaterFrame (ca); Paulo Oliveira (crb). **Getty Images:** torstenvelden (clb). **42 Alamy Stock Photo:** Marevision / agefotostock (cl); Paulo Oliveira (bl). **45 123RF.com:** Sergei Uriadnikov (br). **Alamy Stock Photo:** Nature Picture Library (tc). **46-47 Getty Images / iStock:** E+ / FilippoBacci. **48 123RF.com:** Richard Whitcombe (tr). **Alamy Stock Photo:** Stephen Frink Collection (tl). **48-49 Shutterstock.com:** Rich Carey (bc). **49 Alamy Stock Photo:** Adam Butler (b). **50 Dreamstime.com:** Chee-Onn-Leong (c). **51 Dreamstime.com:** Tatiana Belova (tr, crb); Slowmotiongli (cra); Gorodok495 (cr); Valeronia (br). **52-53 Getty Images:** Paul Starosta. **54 Alamy Stock Photo:** Pablo Méndez / agefotostock (bc/Frog); Wild Wonders of Europe / Hodalic / / Nature Picture Library (bc). **naturepl.com:** D. Parer & E. Parer-Cook (bl). **55 Alamy Stock Photo:** Odilon Dimier / PhotoAlto (clb); Anton Sorokin (cb). **Getty Images / iStock:** AdrianHillman (c). **naturepl.com:** Fred Olivier (fclb). **Shutterstock.com:** Arun Kumar Anantha Kumar (crb). **56 Alamy Stock Photo:** blickwinkel / W. Pattyn (bl). **Ardea:** Phil A. Dotson / Science Source / ardea.com (cla). **Dreamstime.com:** Slowmotiongli (clb); Martin Voeller (tl); Kevin Wells (cl). **58-59 Alamy Stock Photo:** Chris Mattison / Nature Picture Library. **60 123RF.com:** Dirk Ercken (cb, bc/below). **Alamy Stock Photo:** MYN / JP Lawrence / Nature Picture Library (crb). **Dreamstime.com:** Dirk Ercken (br); Dirk Ercken / Kikkerdirk (fbr). **naturepl.com:** Paul Bertner (fcrb); Michael & Patricia Fogden (clb). **61 naturepl.com:** Lucas Bustamante (b). **63 Alamy Stock Photo:** Rich Bunce (tc). **naturepl.com:** Cyril Ruoso (tr). **64-65 Dreamstime.com:** Toldiu74. **66 123RF.com:** Shakeel SM (bc). **Getty Images:** imageBROKER / Michael Weberberger (bc/Sea snake). **Shutterstock.com:** Grzegorz Lukacijewski (bl). **67 Alamy Stock Photo:** A & J Visage (cla); Mike Robinson (cra); Ken Gillespie Photography (tl); Rweisswald (crb). **Vladimir Dinets:** (br). **69 Alamy Stock Photo:** Krystyna Szulecka Photography (tc). **70 Alamy Stock Photo:** Anthony Pierce (bl). **Getty Images:** Mark Deeble and Victoria Stone (br). **73 Alamy Stock Photo:** Claude Thouvenin / Biosphoto (cra); imageBroker / Thorsten Negro (bl). **Science Photo Library:** Frans Lanting, Mint Images (c). **74-75 Shutterstock.com:** NickEvansKZN. **76 Avalon:** Tony Crocetta (bc). **77 Alamy Stock Photo:** Horizon / Horizon International Images Limited (tr); Arco / G. Lacz / Imagebroker (crb); Sibons photography (br). **naturepl.com:** Jen Guyton (cra); Barry Mansell (cr). **79 Dorling Kindersley:** Daniel Long (bl). **Science Photo Library:** Edward Kinsman (clb). **80-81 Getty Images:** jopstock. **82 Alamy Stock Photo:** blickwinkel / McPHOTO / PUM (crb). **Shutterstock.com:** Rachel Portwood (clb). **83 Alamy Stock Photo:** Christine Cuthbertson (crb); Kike Calvo / Alamy Stock Photo (cr); Bob Gibbons (c). **SuperStock:** Jean Paul Ferrero / Pantheon (br). **84 Alamy Stock Photo:** Neil Bowman (cla); imageBROKER / Konrad Wothe (cl). **Dreamstime.com:** Gerfriedscholz (clb). **Getty Images:** Its About Light / Design Pics (tl); Oliver Strewe (bl). **85 Getty Images:** Lisa Mckelvie (br). **86-87 naturepl.com:** Claudio Contreras. **89 Alamy Stock Photo:** Auscape International Pty Ltd / Ian Beattie (cr); Stefano Paterna (tr); NSP-RF (cra); David South (crb). **Dreamstime.com:** Willtu (br). **naturepl.com:** Stefan Christmann (bc). **90 Alamy Stock Photo:** Nature Picture Library / Markus Varesvuo (bl); Prisma by Dukas Presseagentur GmbH / Bernhardt Reiner (br). **91 Getty Images:** DanielBehmPhotography.Com (cb). **92 Taiwanese Photographer Wilson Chen:** (cla, tr). **93 Getty Images:** 500px / David Gruskin (bc). **94-95 Shutterstock.com:** Ondrej Prosicky. **96 Alamy Stock Photo:** Ger Bosma (tl). **Getty Images / iStock:** RNMitra (bl). **97 Alamy Stock Photo:** Blue Planet Archive AAF (bc). **98 Alamy Stock Photo:** Tierfotoagentur / T. Harbig (bl). **99 Alamy Stock Photo:** blickwinkel / H. Kuczka (cra); VWPics / Mario Cea Sanchez (tc). **naturepl.com:** Phil Savoie (br). **100-101 Alamy Stock Photo:** David Carillet. **102 Alamy Stock Photo:** Arco / C. Hütter (bc); Peter M. Wilson (bc/Goats); Robert Haasmann / imageBROKER (bl); Zoonar / Artush Foto (crb). **Dreamstime.com:** Godruma (cra). **103 Alamy Stock Photo:** Sciepro / Science Photo Library (tl); Nature Picture Library (clb). **Shutterstock.com:** Yann hubert (bl); Lab Photo (cb). **104 Ardea:** D. Parer & E. Parer-Cook (clb). **105 Dreamstime.com:** Valentyna Chukhlyebova (tr). **naturepl.com:** Doug Gimesy (bl). **106 Alamy Stock Photo:** Rawy van den Beucken (br). **Dreamstime.com:** Zcello (bl). **107 Alamy Stock Photo:** National Geographic Image Collection (cra). **Dreamstime.com:** Carolina Garcia Aranda (tr); Holly Kuchera (cr); Hotshotsworldwide (crb). **naturepl.com:** Nick Garbutt (br). **109 naturepl.com:** Gabriel Rojo (cra). **110 naturepl.com:** Suzi Eszterhas (bc, br). **111 123RF.com:** vilainecrevette (r). **112 Alamy Stock Photo:** Cathy Withers-Clarke (br). **TurboSquid:** mohannadhisham / Dorling Kindersley (elephant models). **113 Alamy Stock Photo:** AfriPics.com (br); Friedrich von Hörsten (bc). **TurboSquid:** Skazok / Dorling Kindersley (elephant models). **114 123RF.com:** Dmitry Potashkin (bc). **Alamy Stock Photo:** Giedrius Stakauskas (bl). **115 Dreamstime.com:** Isselee (br). **116-117 naturepl.com:** Klein & Hubert. **119 Science Photo Library:** Ken Catania / Visuals Unlimited, Inc (crb). **120 Alamy Stock Photo:** Michele Burgess (clb). **121 Alamy Stock Photo:** Life on white (crb); Nick Garbutt / RGB Ventures / SuperStock (bl). **Dorling Kindersley:** Jerry Young (br). **122 naturepl.com:** Hiroya Minakuchi (br). **123 Alamy Stock Photo:** Diane McAllister / naturepl.com (tr). **naturepl.com:** Konrad Wothe (b). **124 Alamy Stock Photo:** Arco Images / Vnoucek, F / Imagebroker (bl). **125 Dreamstime.com:** Daniel Bellhouse / Danox (tr). **126 naturepl.com:** Thomas Marent (bc). **127 Alamy Stock Photo:** RDW Environmental (clb). **Dreamstime.com:** Sergey Uryadnikov (br). **128 Alamy Stock Photo:** Marius Dobilas (bc). **129 Alamy Stock Photo:** FLPA (cr); Daniel Romero / VWPics (br). **Dreamstime.com:** Kyslynskyy (tl); Slowmotiongli (cra). **131 Alamy Stock Photo:** Andy Rouse / Nature Picture Library (bc). **133 Dorling Kindersley:** Roman Gorielov (bl). **Getty Images:** David Chen / EyeEm (tc). **134-135 naturepl.com:** Laurent Geslin. **136 Getty Images:** Jim Cumming (b). **137 Alamy Stock Photo:** Arco / TUNS / Imagebroker (cb); Werner Layer / mauritius images GmbH (bc). **138 Dreamstime.com:** Outdoorsman (bc). **139 Alamy Stock Photo:** Genevieve Vallee (crb). **140-141 Dreamstime.com:** Matthijs Kuijpers (bc). **140 naturepl.com:** Suzi Eszterhas (bc). **141 FLPA:** Vincent Grafhorst / Minden Pictures (br). **142 Alamy Stock Photo:** Steve Bloom / Steve Bloom Images (c); Photo Researchers / Science History Images (tl). **143 Alamy Stock Photo:** Mint Images / Mint Images Limited (clb). **144 Alamy Stock Photo:** Denis-Huot / Nature Picture Library (bl). **145 Alamy Stock Photo:** Ann & Steve Toon / Nature Picture Library (br). **146 Alamy Stock Photo:** Lena Ivanova (bc). **147 Alamy Stock Photo:** Juniors Bildarchiv / F300 / Juniors Bildarchiv GmbH (bc). **148 Alamy Stock Photo:** Doug Lindstrand / Alaska Stock RF / Design Pics Inc (bl). **149 Getty Images:** Doug Lindstrand / Alaska Stock RF / Design Pics Inc (bc). **Paul Williams:** Paul Williams (tr). **150 Dreamstime.com:** Seanothon (bl). **151 Alamy Stock Photo:** blickwinkel / AGAMI / M. van Duijn (br). **152-153 naturepl.com:** Flip Nicklin.

All other images © Dorling Kindersley
For further information see: www.dkimages.com

**Map data sources:**

**IUCN 2020. The IUCN Red List of Threatened Species. Version 2020-2. https://www.iucnredlist.org:**

**28–29** Butler, M., Cockcroft, A., MacDiarmid, A. & Wahle, R. 2011. *Homarus gammarus*. The IUCN Red List of Threatened Species 2011: e.T169955A69905303. https://dx.doi.org/10.2305/IUCN.UK.2011-1.RLTS.T169955A69905303.en (Common lobster). **42–43** NatureServe. 2013. *Petromyzon marinus*. The IUCN Red List of Threatened Species 2013: e.T16781A18229984. https://dx.doi.org/10.2305/IUCN.UK.2013-1.RLTS.T16781A18229984.en (Sea lamprey). **44–45** Rigby, C.L., Barreto, R., Carlson, J., Fernando, D., Fordham, S., Francis, M.P., Herman, K., Jabado, R.W., Liu, K.M., Lowe, C.G, Marshall, A., Pacoureau, N., Romanov, E., Sherley, R.B. & Winker, H. 2019. *Carcharodon carcharias*. The IUCN Red List of Threatened Species 2019: e.T3855A2878674. https://dx.doi.org/10.2305/IUCN.UK.2019-3.RLTS.T3855A2878674.en (Great white shark). **56–57** IUCN SSC Amphibian Specialist Group. 2015. *Necturus maculosus*. The IUCN Red List of Threatened Species 2015: e.T59433A64731610. https://dx.doi.org/10.2305/IUCN.UK.2015-4.RLTS.T59433A64731610.en (Mudpuppy). **56** Geoffrey Hammerson. 2004. *Amphiuma means*. The IUCN Red List of Threatened Species 2004: e.T59074A11879454. https://dx.doi.org/10.2305/IUCN.UK.2004.RLTS.T59074A11879454.en (Amphiuma); IUCN SSC Amphibian Specialist Group. 2020. *Bolitoglossa mexicana*. The IUCN Red List of Threatened Species 2020: e.T59180A53976360. https://dx.doi.org/10.2305/IUCN.UK.2020-1.RLTS.T59180A53976360.en (Mushroom-tongued salamander); Sergius Kuzmin, Theodore Papenfuss, Max Sparreboom, Ismail H. Ugurtas, Steven Anderson, Trevor Beebee, Mathieu Denoël, Franco Andreone, Brandon Anthony, Benedikt Schmidt, Agnieszka Ogrodowczyk, Maria Ogielska, Jaime Bosch, David Tarkhnishvili, Vladimir Ishchenko. 2009. *Salamandra salamandra*. The IUCN Red List of Threatened Species 2009: e.T59467A11928351. https://dx.doi.org/10.2305/IUCN.UK.2009.RLTS.T59467A11928351.en (Fire salamander); Yoshio Kaneko, Masafumi Matsui. 2004. Andrias japonicus. The IUCN Red List of Threatened Species 2004: e.T1273A3376261. https://dx.doi.

org/10.2305/IUCN.UK.2004.RLTS.T1273A3376261.en (Japanese giant salamander); Jan Willem Arntzen, Sergius Kuzmin, Robert Jehle, Trevor Beebee, David Tarkhnishvili, Vladimir Ishchenko, Natalia Ananjeva, Nikolai Orlov, Boris Tuniyev, Mathieu Denoël, Per Nyström, Brandon Anthony, Benedikt Schmidt, Agnieszka Ogrodowczyk. 2009. *Triturus cristatus*. The IUCN Red List of Threatened Species 2009: e.T22212A9365894. https://dx.doi.org/10.2305/IUCN.UK.2009.RLTS.T22212A9365894.en (Great crested newt). **60–61** IUCN SSC Amphibian Specialist Group. 2015. *Oophaga pumilio*. The IUCN Red List of Threatened Species 2015: e.T55196A3025630. https://dx.doi.org/10.2305/IUCN.UK.2015-4.RLTS.T55196A3025630.en (Strawberry poison dart frog). **62–63** Aram Agasyan, Aziz Avisi, Boris Tuniyev, Jelka Crnobrnja Isailovic, Petros Lymberakis, Claes Andrén, Dan Cogalniceanu, John Wilkinson, Natalia Ananjeva, Nazan Üzüm, Nikolai Orlov, Richard Podloucky, Sako Tuniyev, Uğur Kaya. 2009. *Bufo bufo*. The IUCN Red List of Threatened Species 2009: e.T54596A11159939. https://dx.doi.org/10.2305/IUCN.UK.2009.RLTS.T54596A11159939.en (Common toad). **68–69** Cayot, L.J., Gibbs, J.P., Tapia, W. & Caccone, A. 2017. *Chelonoidis donfaustoi*. The IUCN Red List of Threatened Species 2017: e.T90377132A90377135. https://dx.doi.org/10.2305/IUCN.UK.2017-3.RLTS.T90377132A90377135.en (Eastern Santa Cruz Giant Tortoise); Rhodin, A.G.J., Gibbs, J.P., Cayot, L.J., Kiester, A.R. & Tapia, W. 2017. *Chelonoidis phantasticus* (errata version published in 2018). The IUCN Red List of Threatened Species 2017: e.T170517A128969920. https://dx.doi.org/10.2305/IUCN.UK.2017-3.RLTS.T170517A1315907.en (Fernandina giant tortoise); Caccone, A., Cayot, L.J., Gibbs, J.P. & Tapia, W. 2017. *Chelonoidis becki*. The IUCN Red List of Threatened Species 2017: e.T9018A82426296. https://dx.doi.org/10.2305/IUCN.UK.2017-3.RLTS.T9018A82426296.en (Wolf Volcano giant tortoise); Cayot, L.J., Gibbs, J.P., Tapia, W. & Caccone, A. 2018. *Chelonoidis vandenburghi* (errata version published in 2019). The IUCN Red List of Threatened Species 2018: e.T9027A144766471. https://dx.doi.org/10.2305/IUCN.UK.2018-2.RLTS.T9027A144766471.en (Volcán Alcedo giant tortoise); Cayot, L.J., Gibbs, J.P., Tapia, W. & Caccone, A. 2017. *Chelonoidis porteri*. The IUCN Red List of Threatened Species 2017: e.T9026A82777132. https://dx.doi.org/10.2305/IUCN.UK.2017-3.RLTS.T9026A82777132.en (Western Santa Cruz giant tortoise); Caccone, A., Cayot, L.J., Gibbs, J.P. & Tapia, W. 2017. *Chelonoidis chathamensis*. The IUCN Red List of Threatened Species 2017: e.T9019A82688009. https://dx.doi.org/10.2305/IUCN.UK.2017-3.RLTS.T9019A82688009.en (San Cristóbal giant tortoise); Cayot, L.J., Gibbs, J.P., Tapia, W. & Caccone, A. 2017. *Chelonoidis hoodensis*. The IUCN Red List of Threatened Species 2017: e.T9024A82777079. https://dx.doi.org/10.2305/IUCN.UK.2017-3.RLTS.T9024A82777079.en (Española giant tortoise). **72–73** Jenkins, R.K.B., Andreone, F., Andriamazava, A., Anjeriniaina, M., Brady, L., Glaw, F., Griffiths, R.A., Rabibisoa, N., Rakotomalala, D., Randrianantoandro, J.C., Randrianiriana, J., Randrianizahana, H., Ratsoavina, F. & Robsomanitrandrasana, E. 2011. *Furcifer oustaleti*. The IUCN Red List of Threatened Species 2011: e.T172866A6932058. https://dx.doi.org/10.2305/IUCN.UK.2011-2.RLTS.T172866A6932058.en (Oustalet's chameleon); Jenkins, R.K.B., Andreone, F., Andriamazava, A., Anjeriniaina, M., Brady, L., Glaw, F., Griffiths, R.A., Rabibisoa, N., Rakotomalala, D., Randrianantoandro, J.C., Randrianiriana, J., Randrianizahana, H., Ratsoavina, F. & Robsomanitrandrasana, E. 2011. *Calumma parsonii*. The IUCN Red List of Threatened Species 2011: e.T172896A6937628. https://dx.doi.org/10.2305/IUCN.UK.2011-2.RLTS.T172896A6937628.en (Parson's chameleon); Jenkins, R.K.B., Andreone, F., Andriamazava, A., Anjeriniaina, M., Brady, L., Glaw, F., Griffiths, R.A., Rabibisoa, N., Rakotomalala, D., Randrianantoandro, J.C., Randrianiriana, J., Randrianizahana, H., Ratsoavina, F. & Robsomanitrandrasana, E. 2011. *Furcifer pardalis*. The IUCN Red List of Threatened Species 2011: e.T172955A6947909. https://dx.doi.org/10.2305/IUCN.UK.2011-2.RLTS.T172955A6947909.en (Panther chameleon). **72** Jenkins, R.K.B., Andreone, F., Andriamazava, A., Anjeriniaina, M., Brady, L., Glaw, F., Griffiths, R.A., Rabibisoa, N., Rakotomalala, D., Randrianantoandro, J.C., Randrianiriana, J., Randrianizahana, H., Ratsoavina, F. & Robsomanitrandrasana, E. 2011. *Palleon nasus*. The IUCN Red List of Threatened Species 2011: e.T172773A6915062. https://dx.doi.org/10.2305/IUCN.UK.2011-2.RLTS.T172773A6915062.en (Elongated leaf chameleon); Jenkins, R.K.B., Andreone, F., Andriamazava, A., Anjeriniaina, M., Brady, L., Glaw, F., Griffiths, R.A., Rabibisoa, N., Rakotomalala, D., Randrianantoandro, J.C., Randrianiriana, J., Randrianizahana , H., Ratsoavina, F. & Robsomanitrandrasana, E. 2011. *Furcifer labordi*. The IUCN Red List of Threatened Species 2011: e.T8765A12929754. https://dx.doi.org/10.2305/IUCN.UK.2011-2.RLTS.T8765A12929754.en (Laborde's chameleon). **77** Stuart, B., Nguyen, T.Q., Thy, N., Grismer, L., Chan-Ard, T., Iskandar, D., Golynsky, E. & Lau, M.W.N. 2012. *Python bivittatus* (errata version published in 2019). The IUCN Red List of Threatened Species 2012: e.T193451A151341916. https://dx.doi.org/10.2305/IUCN.UK.2012-1.RLTS.T193451A151341916.en (Burmese python); Stuart, B., Thy, N., Chan-Ard, T., Nguyen, T.Q., Grismer, L., Auliya, M., Das, I. & Wogan, G. 2018. *Python reticulatus*. The IUCN Red List of Threatened Species 2018: e.T183151A1730027. https://dx.doi.org/10.2305/IUCN.UK.2018-2.RLTS.T183151A1730027.en (Reticulated python); Tallowin, O., Allison, A., Parker, F. & O'Shea, M. 2017. *Morelia amethistina*. The IUCN Red List of Threatened Species 2017: e.T177501A1489667. https://dx.doi.org/10.2305/IUCN.UK.2017-3.RLTS.T177501A1489667.en (Amethystine python). **78–79** Spawls, S. 2010. *Dendroaspis polylepis*. The IUCN Red List of Threatened Species 2010: e.T177584A7461853. https://dx.doi.org/10.2305/IUCN.UK.2010-4.RLTS.T177584A7461853.en (Black mamba); Frost, D.R., Hammerson, G.A. & Santos-Barrera, G. 2007. *Crotalus atrox*. The IUCN Red List of Threatened Species 2007: e.T64311A12763519. https://dx.doi.org/10.2305/IUCN.UK.2007.RLTS.T64311A12763519.en (Diamond-backed rattlesnake); Ji, X., Rao, D.-q. & Wang, Y. 2012. *Bungarus multicinctus*. The IUCN Red List of Threatened Species 2012: e.T191957A2020937. https://dx.doi.org/10.2305/IUCN.UK.2012-1.RLTS.T191957A2020937.en (Many-banded krait); Michael, D., Clemann, N. & Robertson, P. 2018. *Notechis scutatus*. The IUCN Red List of Threatened Species 2018: e.T169687A83767147. https://dx.doi.org/10.2305/IUCN.UK.2018-1.RLTS.T169687A83767147.en (Tiger snake). **84–85** BirdLife International. 2018. *Struthio camelus*. The IUCN Red List of Threatened Species 2018: e.T45020636A132189458. https://dx.doi.org/10.2305/IUCN.UK.2018-2.RLTS.T45020636A132189458.en (Common Ostrich, Somali ostrich); BirdLife International. 2016. *Struthio molybdophanes*. The IUCN Red List of Threatened Species 2016: e.T22732795A95049558. https://dx.doi.org/10.2305/IUCN.UK.2016-3.RLTS.T22732795A95049558.en (Common Ostrich, Somali ostrich). **84** BirdLife International. 2020. *Rhea tarapacensis*. The IUCN Red List of Threatened Species 2020: e.T22728206A177987446 (Puna rhea); BirdLife International. 2017. *Casuarius unappendiculatus*. The IUCN Red List of Threatened Species 2017: e.T22678114A118134784. https://dx.doi.org/10.2305/IUCN.UK.2017-3.RLTS.T22678114A118134784.en (Northern cassowary); BirdLife International. 2018. *Dromaius novaehollandiae*. The IUCN Red List of Threatened Species 2018: e.T22678117A131902466. https://dx.doi.org/10.2305/IUCN.UK.2018-2.RLTS.T22678117A131902466.en (Common emu). **88–89** BirdLife International. 2018. *Aptenodytes forsteri*. The IUCN Red List of Threatened Species 2018: e.T22697752A132600320. https://dx.doi.org/10.2305/IUCN.UK.2018-2.RLTS.T22697752A132600320.en (Emperor Penguin). **89** BirdLife International. 2018. *Pygoscelis adeliae*. The IUCN Red List of Threatened Species 2018: e.T22697758A132601165. https://dx.doi.org/10.2305/IUCN.UK.2018-2.RLTS.T22697758A132601165.en (Adelie penguin); BirdLife International. 2018. *Spheniscus mendiculus*. The IUCN Red List of Threatened Species 2018: e.T22697825A132606008. https://dx.doi.org/10.2305/IUCN.UK.2018-2.RLTS.T22697825A132606008.en (Galapagos penguin); BirdLife International. 2018. *Spheniscus demersus*. The IUCN Red List of Threatened Species 2018: e.T22697810A132604504. https://dx.doi.org/10.2305/IUCN.UK.2018-2.RLTS.T22697810A132604504.en (Jackass penguin); BirdLife International. 2018. *Eudyptula minor*. The IUCN Red List of Threatened Species 2018: e.T22697805A132603951. https://dx.doi.org/10.2305/IUCN.UK.2018-2.RLTS.T22697805A132603951.en (Little penguin); BirdLife International. 2018. *Eudyptes chrysolophus*. The IUCN Red List of Threatened Species 2018: e.T22697793A132602631. https://dx.doi.org/10.2305/IUCN.UK.2018-2.RLTS.T22697793A132602631.en (Macaroni penguin). **90–91** BirdLife International. 2017. *Bubo scandiacus* (errata version published in 2018). The IUCN Red List of Threatened Species 2017: e.T22689055A127837214. https://dx.doi.org/10.2305/IUCN.UK.2017-3.RLTS.T22689055A119342767.en (Snowy owl). **92–93** BirdLife International. 2019. *Pandion haliaetus* (amended version of 2016 assessment). The IUCN Red List of Threatened Species 2019: e.T22694938A155519951. https://dx.doi.org/10.2305/IUCN.UK.2019-3.RLTS.T22694938A155519951.en (Osprey). **96–97** BirdLife International. 2018. *Ara ararauna*. The IUCN Red List of Threatened Species 2018: e.T22685539A131917270. https://dx.doi.org/10.2305/IUCN.UK.2018-2.RLTS.T22685539A131917270.en (Blue-and-yellow macaw). **98–99** BirdLife International. 2019. *Hirundo rustica*. The IUCN Red List of Threatened Species 2019: e.T22712252A137668645. https://dx.doi.org/10.2305/IUCN.UK.2019-3.RLTS.T22712252A137668645.en (Barn swallow). **104–105** Leary, T., Seri, L., Flannery, T., Wright, D., Hamilton, S., Helgen, K., Singadan, R., Menzies, J., Allison, A., James, R., Aplin, K., Salas, L. & Dickman, C. 2016. *Zaglossus bartoni*. The IUCN Red List of Threatened Species 2016: e.T136552A21964496. https://dx.doi.org/10.2305/IUCN.UK.2016-2.RLTS.T136552A21964496.en (Eastern long-beaked echidna); Leary, T., Seri, L., Flannery, T., Wright, D., Hamilton, S., Helgen, K., Singadan, R., Menzies, J., Allison, A., James, R., Aplin, K., Salas, L. & Dickman, C. 2016. *Zaglossus bruijnii*. The IUCN Red List of Threatened Species 2016: e.T23179A21964204. https://dx.doi.org/10.2305/IUCN.UK.2016-2.RLTS.T23179A21964204.en (Western long-beaked echidna); Aplin, K., Dickman, C., Salas, L. & Helgen, K. 2016. *Tachyglossus aculeatus*. The IUCN Red List of Threatened Species 2016: e.T41312A21964662. https://dx.doi.org/10.2305/IUCN.UK.2016-2.RLTS.T41312A21964662.en (Short-beaked echidna); Woinarski, J. & Burbidge, A.A. 2016. *Ornithorhynchus anatinus*. The IUCN Red List of Threatened Species 2016: e.T40488A21964009. https://dx.doi.org/10.2305/IUCN.UK.2016-1.RLTS.T40488A21964009.en (Platypus). **106–107** Woinarski, J. & Burbidge, A.A. 2020. *Phascolarctos cinereus* (amended version of 2016 assessment). The IUCN Red List of Threatened Species 2020: e.T16892A166496779. https://dx.doi.org/10.2305/IUCN.UK.2020-1.RLTS.T16892A166496779.en (Koala). **107** Salas, L., Dickman, C., Helgen, K. & Flannery, T. 2019. *Ailurops ursinus*. The IUCN Red List of Threatened Species 2019: e.T40637A21949654. https://dx.doi.org/10.2305/IUCN.UK.2019-1.RLTS.T40637A21949654.en (Bear cuscus); Ellis, M., van Weenen, J., Copley, P., Dickman, C., Mawson, P. & Woinarski, J. 2016. *Macropus rufus*. The IUCN Red List of Threatened Species 2016: e.T40567A21953534. https://dx.doi.org/10.2305/IUCN.UK.2016-2.RLTS.T40567A21953534.en (Red kangaroo); Pérez-Hernandez, R., Lew, D. & Solari, S. 2016. *Didelphis virginiana*. The IUCN Red List of Threatened Species 2016: e.T40502A22176259. https://dx.doi.org/10.2305/IUCN.UK.2016-1.RLTS.T40502A22176259.en (Virginia opossum); Hawkins, C.E., McCallum, H., Mooney, N., Jones, M. & Holdsworth, M. 2008. *Sarcophilus harrisii*. The IUCN Red List of Threatened Species 2008: e.T40540A10331066. https://dx.doi.org/10.2305/IUCN.UK.2008.RLTS.T40540A10331066.en (Tasmanian devil); Leary, T., Seri, L., Wright, D., Hamilton, S., Helgen, K., Singadan, R., Menzies, J., Allison, A., James, R., Dickman, C., Aplin, K., Flannery, T., Martin, R. & Salas, L. 2016. *Dendrolagus goodfellowi*. The IUCN Red List of Threatened Species 2016: e.T6429A21957524. https://dx.doi.org/10.2305/IUCN.UK.2016-2.RLTS.T6429A21957524.en (Tree kangaroo). **108–109** Anacleto, T.C.S., Miranda, F., Medri, I., Cuellar, E., Abba, A.M. & Superina, M. 2014. *Priodontes maximus*. The IUCN Red List of Threatened Species 2014: e.T18144A47442343. https://dx.doi.org/10.2305/IUCN.UK.2014-1.RLTS.T18144A47442343.en (Giant armadillo); Loughry, J., McDonough, C. & Abba, A.M. 2014. *Dasypus novemcinctus*. The IUCN Red List of Threatened Species 2014: e.T6290A47440785. https://dx.doi.org/10.2305/IUCN.UK.2014-1.RLTS.T6290A47440785.en (Nine-banded armadillo); Superina, M. & Abba, A.M. 2014. *Dasypus pilosus*. The IUCN Red List of Threatened Species 2014: e.T6291A47441122. https://dx.doi.org/10.2305/IUCN.UK.2014-1.RLTS.T6291A47441122.en (Hairy long-nosed armadillo); Superina, M., Abba, A.M. & Roig, V.G. 2014. *Chlamyphorus truncatus*. The IUCN Red List of Threatened Species 2014: e.T4704A47439264. https://dx.doi.org/10.2305/IUCN.UK.2014-1.RLTS.T4704A47439264.en (Pink fairy armadillo); Noss, A., Superina, M. & Abba, A.M. 2014. *Tolypeutes matacus*. The IUCN Red List of Threatened Species 2014: e.T21974A47443233. https://dx.doi.org/10.2305/IUCN.UK.2014-1.RLTS.T21974A47443233.en (Southern three-banded armadillo).

**110–111** Moraes-Barros, N., Chiarello, A. & Plese, T. 2014. *Bradypus variegatus*. The IUCN Red List of Threatened Species 2014: e. T3038A47437046. https://dx.doi.org/10.2305/IUCN.UK.2014-1.RLTS.T3038A47437046.en (Brown-throated sloth). **112–113** Blanc, J. 2008. *Loxodonta africana*. The IUCN Red List of Threatened Species 2008: e.T12392A3339343. https://dx.doi.org/10.2305/IUCN.UK.2008.RLTS.T12392A3339343.en (African forest elephant & African savannah elephant); Choudhury, A., Lahiri Choudhury, D.K., Desai, A., Duckworth, J.W., Easa, P.S., Johnsingh, A.J.T., Fernando, P., Hedges, S., Gunawardena, M., Kurt, F., Karanth, U., Lister, A., Menon, V., Riddle, H., Rübel, A. & Wikramanayake, E. (IUCN SSC Asian Elephant Specialist Group). 2008. *Elephas maximus*. The IUCN Red List of Threatened Species 2008: e.T7140A12828813. https://dx.doi.org/10.2305/IUCN.UK.2008.RLTS.T7140A12828813.en (Asian elephant). **114–115** Shar, S., Lkhagvasuren, D., Bertolino, S., Henttonen, H., Kryštufek, B. & Meinig, H. 2016. *Sciurus vulgaris* (errata version published in 2017). The IUCN Red List of Threatened Species 2016: e. T20025A115155900. https://dx.doi.org/10.2305/IUCN.UK.2016-3.RLTS.T20025A22245887.en (Eurasian red squirrel). **118–119** Cassola, F. 2016. *Condylura cristata* (errata version published in 2017). The IUCN Red List of Threatened Species 2016: e. T41458A115187740. https://dx.doi.org/10.2305/IUCN.UK.2016-3.RLTS.T41458A22322697.en (Star-nosed mole). **120–121** Louis, E.E., Sefczek, T.M., Randimbiharinirina, D.R., Raharivololona, B., Rakotondrazandry, J.N., Manjary, D., Aylward, M. & Ravelomandrato, F. 2020. *Daubentonia madagascariensis*. The IUCN Red List of Threatened Species 2020: e.T6302A115560793. https://dx.doi.org/10.2305/IUCN.UK.2020-2.RLTS.T6302A115560793.en (Aye-aye); LaFleur, M. & Gould, L. 2020. *Lemur catta*. The IUCN Red List of Threatened Species 2020: e. T11496A115565760. https://dx.doi.org/10.2305/IUCN.UK.2020-2.RLTS.T11496A115565760.en (Ring-tailed lemur); Louis, E.E., Sefczek, T.M., Bailey, C.A., Raharivololona, B., Lewis, R. & Rakotomalala, E.J. 2020. *Propithecus verreauxi*. The IUCN Red List of Threatened Species 2020: e.T18354A115572044. https://dx.doi.org/10.2305/IUCN.UK.2020-2.RLTS.T18354A115572044.en (Verreaux's sifaka); Louis, E.E., Bailey, C.A., Frasier, C.L., Raharivololona, B., Schwitzer, C., Ratsimbazafy, J., Wilmet, L., Lewis, R. & Rakotomalala, D. 2020. *Lepilemur ruficaudatus*. The IUCN Red List of Threatened Species 2020: e. T11621A115566869. https://dx.doi.org/10.2305/IUCN.UK.2020-2.RLTS.T11621A115566869.en (Ring-tailed lemur); Blanco, M., Dolch, R., Ganzhorn, J., Greene, L.K., Le Pors, B., Lewis, R., Louis, E.E., Rafalinirina, H.A., Raharivololona, B., Rakotoarisoa, G., Ralison, J., Randriahaingo, H.N.T., Rasoloarison, R.M., Razafindrasolo, M., Sgarlata, G.M., Wright, P. & Zaonarivelo, J. 2020. *Cheirogaleus medius*. The IUCN Red List of Threatened Species 2020: e. T163023599A115588562. https://dx.doi.org/10.2305/IUCN.UK.2020-2.RLTS.T163023599A115588562.en (Fat-tailed dwarf lemur). **122–123** Watanabe, K. & Tokita, K. 2020. *Macaca fuscata*. The IUCN Red List of Threatened Species 2020: e.T12552A17949359. https://dx.doi.org/10.2305/IUCN.UK.2020-2.RLTS.T12552A17949359.en (Japanese macaque). **124–125** Fruth, B., Hickey, J.R., André, C., Furuichi, T., Hart, J., Hart, T., Kuehl, H., Maisels, F., Nackoney, J., Reinartz, G., Sop, T., Thompson, J. & Williamson, E.A. 2016. *Pan paniscus* (errata version published in 2016). The IUCN Red List of Threatened Species 2016: e. T15932A102331567. https://dx.doi.org/10.2305/IUCN.UK.2016-2.RLTS.T15932A17964305.en (Bonobo); Maisels, F., Bergl, R.A. & Williamson, E.A. 2018. *Gorilla gorilla* (amended version of 2016 assessment). The IUCN Red List of Threatened Species 2018: e.T9404A136250858. https://dx.doi.org/10.2305/IUCN.UK.2018-2.RLTS.T9404A136250858.en (Western gorilla); Plumptre, A., Robbins, M.M. & Williamson, E.A. 2019. *Gorilla beringei*. The IUCN Red List of Threatened Species 2019: e. T39994A115576640. https://dx.doi.org/10.2305/IUCN.UK.2019-1.RLTS.T39994A115576640.en (Eastern gorilla); Humle, T., Maisels, F., Oates, J.F., Plumptre, A. & Williamson, E.A. 2016. *Pan troglodytes* (errata version published in 2018). The IUCN Red List of Threatened Species 2016: e.T15933A129038584. https://dx.doi.org/10.2305/IUCN.UK.2016-2.RLTS.T15933A17964454.en (Chimpanzee). **126–127** Ancrenaz, M., Gumal, M., Marshall, A.J., Meijaard, E., Wich, S.A. & Husson, S. 2016. *Pongo pygmaeus* (errata version published in 2018). The IUCN Red List of Threatened Species 2016: e.T17975A123809220. https://dx.doi.org/10.2305/IUCN.UK.2016-1.RLTS.T17975A17966347.en (Bornean orangutan); Singleton, I., Wich, S.A., Nowak, M., Usher, G. & Utami-Atmoko, S.S. 2017. *Pongo abelii* (errata version published in 2018). The IUCN Red List of Threatened Species 2017: e. T121097935A123797627. https://dx.doi.org/10.2305/IUCN.UK.2017-3.RLTS.T121097935A115575085.en (Sumatran orangutan); Nowak, M.G., Rianti, P., Wich, S.A., Meijaard, E. & Fredriksson, G. 2017. *Pongo tapanuliensis*. The IUCN Red List of Threatened Species 2017: e.T120588639A120588662. https://dx.doi.org/10.2305/IUCN.UK.2017-3.RLTS.T120588639A120588662.en (Tapanuli orangutan). **128–129** Molur, S., Srinivasulu, C., Bates, P. & Francis, C. 2008. *Pteropus giganteus*. The IUCN Red List of Threatened Species 2008: e.T18725A8511108. https://dx.doi.org/10.2305/IUCN.UK.2008.RLTS.T18725A8511108.en (Indian flying fox). **129** Armstrong, K.D., Woinarski, J.C.Z., Hanrahan, N.M. & Burbidge, A.A. 2019. *Macroderma gigas*. The IUCN Red List of Threatened Species 2019: e.T12590A22027714. https://dx.doi.org/10.2305/IUCN.UK.2019-3.RLTS.T12590A22027714.en (Ghost false vampire bat); Bates, P., Bumrungsri, S. & Francis, C. 2019. *Craseonycteris thonglongyai*. The IUCN Red List of Threatened Species 2019: e. T5481A22072935. https://dx.doi.org/10.2305/IUCN.UK.2019-3.RLTS.T5481A22072935.en (Hog-nosed bat); Piraccini, R. 2016. *Rhinolophus ferrumequinum*. The IUCN Red List of Threatened Species 2016: e.T19517A21973253. https://dx.doi.org/10.2305/IUCN.UK.2016-2.RLTS.T19517A21973253.en (Greater horseshoe bat); O'Donnell, C. 2008. *Mystacina tuberculata*. The IUCN Red List of Threatened Species 2008: e. T14261A4427784. https://dx.doi.org/10.2305/IUCN.UK.2008.RLTS.T14261A4427784.en (New Zealand (lesser) short-tailed bat); O'Donnell, C. 2008. *Mystacina robusta*. The IUCN Red List of Threatened Species 2008: e.T14260A4427606. https://dx.doi.org/10.2305/IUCN.UK.2008.RLTS.T14260A4427606.en (New Zealand (greater) short-tailed bat); Monadjem, A., Cardiff, S.G., Rakotoarivelo, A.R., Jenkins, R.K.B. & Ratrimomanarivo, F.H. 2017. *Myzopoda aurita*. The IUCN Red List of Threatened Species 2017: e.T14288A22073303. https://dx.doi.org/10.2305/IUCN.UK.2017-2.RLTS.T14288A22073303.en (Madagascar sucker-footed bat); Barquez, R., Perez, S., Miller, B. & Diaz, M. 2015. *Diaemus youngi*. The IUCN Red List of Threatened Species 2015: e. T6520A21982777. https://dx.doi.org/10.2305/IUCN.UK.2015-4.RLTS.T6520A21982777.en (White-winged vampire bat). **130–131** Goodrich, J., Lynam, A., Miquelle, D., Wibisono, H., Kawanishi, K., Pattanavibool, A., Htun, S., Tempa, T., Karki, J., Jhala, Y. & Karanth, U. 2015. *Panthera tigris*. The IUCN Red List of Threatened Species 2015: e.T15955A50659951. https://dx.doi.org/10.2305/IUCN.UK.2015-2.RLTS.T15955A50659951.en (Tiger). **132–133** Bauer, H., Packer, C., Funston, P.F., Henschel, P. & Nowell, K. 2016. *Panthera leo* (errata version published in 2017). The IUCN Red List of Threatened Species 2016: e.T15951A115130419. https://dx.doi.org/10.2305/IUCN.UK.2016-3.RLTS.T15951A107265605.en (Lion). **136–137** Boitani, L., Phillips, M. & Jhala, Y. 2018. *Canis lupus* (errata version published in 2020). The IUCN Red List of Threatened Species 2018: e. T3746A163508960. https://dx.doi.org/10.2305/IUCN.UK.2018-2.RLTS.T3746A163508960.en (Grey wolf). **138–139** Garshelis, D.L., Scheick, B.K., Doan-Crider, D.L., Beecham, J.J. & Obbard, M.E. 2016. *Ursus americanus* (errata version published in 2017). The IUCN Red List of Threatened Species 2016: e. T41687A114251609. https://dx.doi.org/10.2305/IUCN.UK.2016-3.RLTS.T41687A45034604.en (American black bear); Wiig, Ø., Amstrup, S., Atwood, T., Laidre, K., Lunn, N., Obbard, M., Regehr, E. & Thiemann, G. 2015. *Ursus maritimus*. The IUCN Red List of Threatened Species 2015: e.T22823A14871490. https://dx.doi.org/10.2305/IUCN.UK.2015-4.RLTS.T22823A14871490.en (Polar bear); Swaisgood, R., Wang, D. & Wei, F. 2016. *Ailuropoda melanoleuca* (errata version published in 2017). The IUCN Red List of Threatened Species 2016: e.T712A121745669. https://dx.doi.org/10.2305/IUCN.UK.2016-2.RLTS.T712A45033386.en (Giant panda); McLellan, B.N., Proctor, M.F., Huber, D. & Michel, S. 2017. *Ursus arctos* (amended version of 2017 assessment). The IUCN Red List of Threatened Species 2017: e. T41688A121229971. https://dx.doi.org/10.2305/IUCN.UK.2017-3.RLTS.T41688A121229971.en (Brown bear); Garshelis, D. & Steinmetz, R. 2016. *Ursus thibetanus* (errata version published in 2017). The IUCN Red List of Threatened Species 2016: e.T22824A114252336. https://dx.doi.org/10.2305/IUCN.UK.2016-3.RLTS.T22824A45034242.en (Asiatic black bear); Scotson, L., Fredriksson, G., Augeri, D., Cheah, C., Ngoprasert, D. & Wai-Ming, W. 2017. *Helarctos malayanus* (errata version published in 2018). The IUCN Red List of Threatened Species 2017: e.T9760A123798233. https://dx.doi.org/10.2305/IUCN.UK.2017-3.RLTS.T9760A45033547.en (Sun bear); Dharaiya, N., Bargali, H.S. & Sharp, T. 2020. *Melursus ursinus* (amended version of 2016 assessment). The IUCN Red List of Threatened Species 2020: e. T13143A166519315. https://dx.doi.org/10.2305/IUCN.UK.2020-1.RLTS.T13143A166519315.en (Sloth bear); Velez-Liendo, X. & García-Rangel, S. 2017. *Tremarctos ornatus* (errata version published in 2018). The IUCN Red List of Threatened Species 2017: e. T22066A123792952. https://dx.doi.org/10.2305/IUCN.UK.2017-3.RLTS.T22066A45034047.en (Spectacled bear). **140–141** Do Linh San, E., Begg, C., Begg, K. & Abramov, A.V. 2016. *Mellivora capensis*. The IUCN Red List of Threatened Species 2016: e.T41629A45210107. https://dx.doi.org/10.2305/IUCN.UK.2016-1.RLTS.T41629A45210107.en (Honey badger). **142–143** Rubenstein, D., Low Mackey, B., Davidson, ZD, Kebede, F. & King, S.R.B. 2016. *Equus grevyi*. The IUCN Red List of Threatened Species 2016: e.T7950A89624491. https://dx.doi.org/10.2305/IUCN.UK.2016-3.RLTS.T7950A89624491.en (Grevy's zebra); King, S.R.B. & Moehlman, P.D. 2016. *Equus quagga*. The IUCN Red List of Threatened Species 2016: e. T41013A45172424. https://dx.doi.org/10.2305/IUCN.UK.2016-2.RLTS.T41013A45172424.en (Plains zebra); Gosling, L.M., Muntifering, J., Kolberg, H., Uiseb, K. & King, S.R.B. 2019. *Equus zebra* (amended version of 2019 assessment). The IUCN Red List of Threatened Species 2019: e.T7960A160755590. https://dx.doi.org/10.2305/IUCN.UK.2019-1.RLTS.T7960A160755590.en (Mountain zebra). **144–145** Emslie, R. 2020. *Diceros bicornis*. The IUCN Red List of Threatened Species 2020: e. T6557A152728945. https://dx.doi.org/10.2305/IUCN.UK.2020-1.RLTS.T6557A152728945.en (Black rhino); Emslie, R. 2020. *Ceratotherium simum*. The IUCN Red List of Threatened Species 2020: e.T4185A45813880. https://dx.doi.org/10.2305/IUCN.UK.2020-1.RLTS.T4185A45813880.en (White rhino); Ellis, S. & Talukdar, B. 2019. *Rhinoceros unicornis*. The IUCN Red List of Threatened Species 2019: e. T19496A18494149. https://dx.doi.org/10.2305/IUCN.UK.2019-3.RLTS.T19496A18494149.en (One-horned rhino). **146–147** Lewison, R. & Pluháček, J. 2017. *Hippopotamus amphibius*. The IUCN Red List of Threatened Species 2017: e. T10103A18567364. https://dx.doi.org/10.2305/IUCN.UK.2017-2.RLTS.T10103A18567364.en (Hippopotamus); Ransom, C, Robinson, P.T. & Collen, B. 2015. *Choeropsis liberiensis*. The IUCN Red List of Threatened Species 2015: e. T10032A18567171. https://dx.doi.org/10.2305/IUCN.UK.2015-2.RLTS.T10032A18567171.en (Pygmy hippo). **148–149** Hundertmark, K. 2016. *Alces alces*. The IUCN Red List of Threatened Species 2016: e.T56003281A22157381. https://dx.doi.org/10.2305/IUCN.UK.2016-1.RLTS.T56003281A22157381.en (Moose). **150–151** Cooke, J.G. 2018. *Megaptera novaeangliae*. The IUCN Red List of Threatened Species 2018: e. T13006A50362794. https://dx.doi.org/10.2305/IUCN.UK.2018-2.RLTS.T13006A50362794.en (Humpback whale).

**Other Data Credits:**

**26–27** Food and Agriculture Organization of the United Nations.
**30–31** The Genetics Society of America (GSA): The Functional Basis of Wing Patterning in Heliconius Butterflies: The Molecules Behind Mimicry, Marcus R. Kronforst and Riccardo Papa, GENETICS May 1, 2015 vol. 200 no. 1 1-19; https://doi.org/10.1534/genetics.114.172387 / Copyright Clearance Center - Rightslink.
**34–35** World Spider Catalog (2020). World Spider Catalog. Version 21.5.
**36–37** Aquamaps: Computer generated distribution maps for Asterias rubens (common starfish), with mode lled year 2050 native range map based on IPCC RCP8.5 emissions scenario. www.aquamaps.org, version 10 / 2019. Accessed 12 Oct. 2020.
**42–43** This map was retrieved, with permission, from www.fishbase.org/summary/Petromyzon-marinus.html.
**48–49** Aquamaps: Scarponi, P., G. Coro, and P. Pagano. A collection of Aquamaps native layers in NetCDF format. Data in brief 17 (2018): 292-296.
**50–51** Multidisciplinary Digital Publishing Institute.
**68** Rune Midtgaard, RepFocus (www.repfocus.dk)
**70–71** Rune Midtgaard, RepFocus (www.repfocus.dk).
**76–77** Rune Midtgaard, RepFocus (www.repfocus.dk).
**79** Rune Midtgaard, RepFocus (www.repfocus.dk).
**88–89** Elsevier.
**132–133** PLOS Genetics.
**137** Wikipedia: (Dingo).
**150–151** NOAA.

ARCTIC OCEAN

Chukchi Sea
Beaufort Sea
Queen Elizabeth Islands
Ellesmere Island
Greenland
Greenland Sea

Bering Strait
Brooks Range
Yukon
Mackenzie
Victoria Island
Baffin Island
Baffin Bay
Norwegian Sea

Bering Sea
△ Denali (Mount McKinley) 6,194 m (20,320 ft)
Great Bear Lake
Great Slave Lake
Hudson Bay
Davis Strait
Denmark Strait
Iceland
North Sea

Aleutian Basin
Aleutian Islands
Aleutian Trench
Gulf of Alaska
Coast Mountains
Rocky Mountains
Canadian Shield
Laurentian Mountains
Labrador Sea
British Isles

Vancouver Island
NORTH AMERICA
Great Lakes
EU
A

Mendocino Fracture Zone
Missouri
Great Plains
Appalachian Mts
North American Basin
Azores
Iberian Peninsula
Medite

Murray Fracture Zone
Sierra Madre Occidental
Sierra Madre Oriental
Mississippi
Madeira
Atlas Mountains

Hawaiian Islands
Clarion Fracture Zone
Gulf of Mexico
West Indies
Greater Antilles
Canary Islands
Ahaggar
Sahar

Hawaii
Yucatán Peninsula
Caribbean Sea
Lesser Antilles
Cape Verde Islands
S a h e l
Niger
A

Line Islands
Clipperton Fracture Zone
Middle America Trench
Orinoco
Guiana Highlands
ATLANTIC
Gulf of Guinea

Polynesia
Kiritimati
PACIFIC
Galápagos Islands
Amazon
Amazon Basin
SOUTH AMERICA
OCEAN

OCEAN
Peru-Chile Trench
Andes
Brazil Basin
Angola Basin

Marquesas Islands
Peru Basin
Planalto de Mato Grosso
Brazilian Highlands

Tuamotu Islands
Nazca Ridge
Gran Chaco
Rio Grande Rise

Pitcairn Island
Sala y Gomez Ridge
Paraná

Tubuai Islands
Easter Island
Roggeveen Basin
Aconcagua △ 6,959 m (22,837 ft)
Andes
Pampas
Argentine Basin
Cape Basin

East Pacific Rise
Southwest Pacific Basin
Patagonia

Eltanin Fracture Zone
Falkland Islands
Mid-Atlantic Ridge

Tierra del Fuego
South Georgia

Cape Horn
Scotia Sea
America-Antarctic Ridge

KEY
△ mountain
river

Drake Passage

Southeast Pacific Basin
Antarctic Peninsula

Bellinghausen Sea
Weddell Plain
Weddell Sea

SO